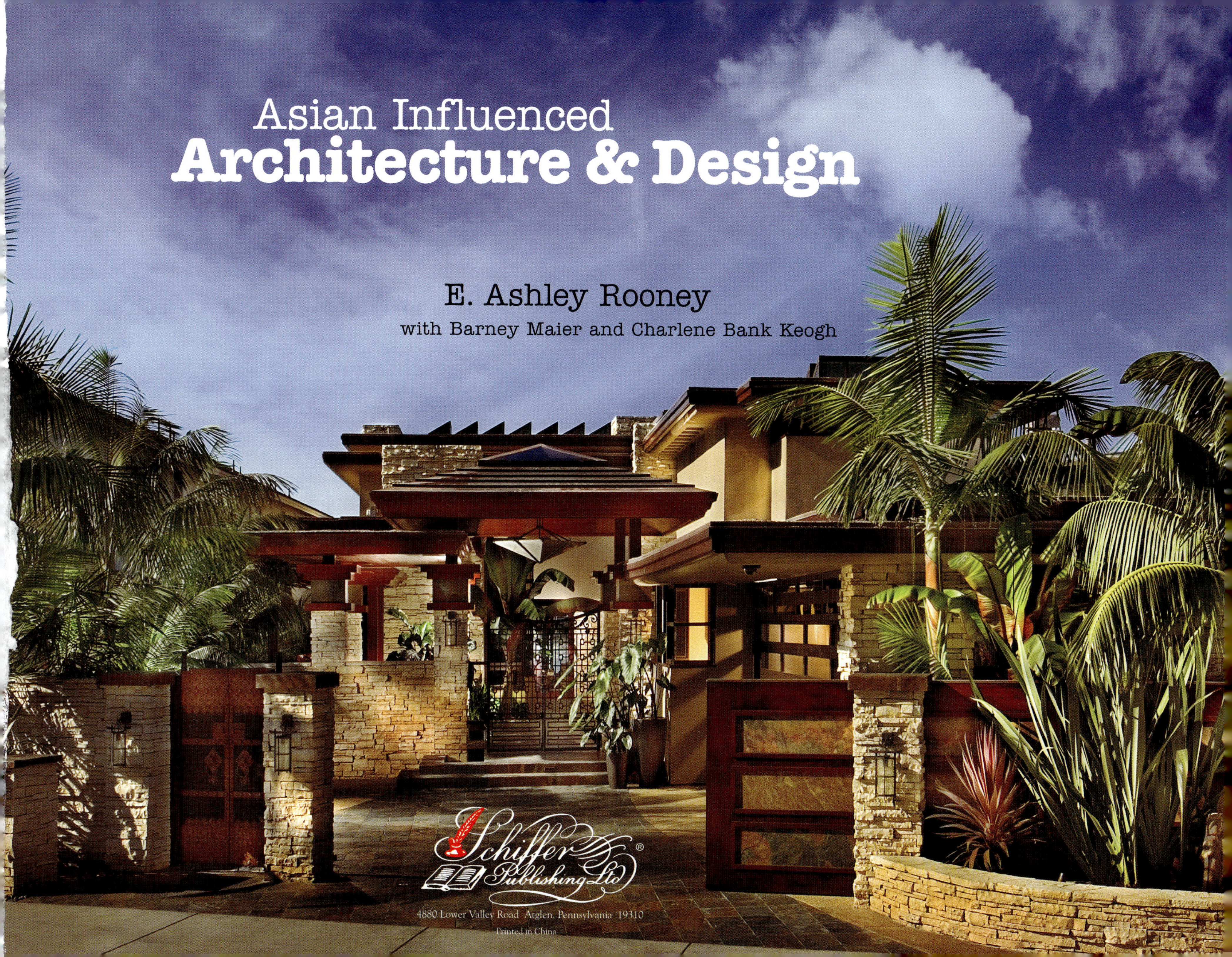

Asian Influenced
Architecture & Design

E. Ashley Rooney

with Barney Maier and Charlene Bank Keogh

Schiffer Publishing Ltd®

4880 Lower Valley Road Atglen, Pennsylvania 19310

Printed in China

ACKNOWLEDGMENTS

I consider myself most fortunate to have worked with Tina Skinner of Schiffer Publishing for all these years. She prods me when I need prodding and laughs when I need joy.

I also must thank Bob and Jane Carpenter, Joan and Bill Ford, Tuulikki Loring, Tricia Traxler, and Pan Zhai who made many contributions to this work. Manish Dikshit, partner and design principal of Aum Architects, a Mumbai-based architectural and interior designing firm, with a vast expertise in both residential and commercial interior spaces in Asia, played a significant role in the creation of this book.

Library of Congress Control Number: 2009942242

Covers and book designed by: Bruce Waters
Type set in Zurich BT

ISBN: 978-0-7643-3383-5
Printed in China

Schiffer Books are available at special discounts for bulk purchases for sales promotions or premiums. Special editions, including personalized covers, corporate imprints, and excerpts can be created in large quantities for special needs. For more information contact the publisher:

Photo credits:
Front cover: James Abts, Hamilton, Massachusetts; inset photo by Eric Figge Photography
Spine: John Ellis
Back cover: upper left courtesy of ©2008mcconnellphoto.net; lower left courtesy of Estelle G. Jaivin ASID, CID; upper right: © Paul Bardagjy; lower right: John Horner
Title page: Eric Figge Photography

Published by Schiffer Publishing Ltd.
4880 Lower Valley Road
Atglen, PA 19310
Phone: (610) 593-1777; Fax: (610) 593-2002
E-mail: Info@schifferbooks.com

For the largest selection of fine reference books on this and related subjects, please visit our web site at **www.schifferbooks.com**
We are always looking for people to write books on new and related subjects. If you have an idea for a book please contact us at the above address.

This book may be purchased from the publisher.
Include $5.00 for shipping.
Please try your bookstore first.
You may write for a free catalog.

In Europe, Schiffer books are distributed by
Bushwood Books
6 Marksbury Ave.
Kew Gardens
Surrey TW9 4JF England
Phone: 44 (0) 20 8392 8585; Fax: 44 (0) 20 8392 9876
E-mail: info@bushwoodbooks.co.uk
Website: www.bushwoodbooks.co.uk

CONTENTS

Photo: John Ellis

1. Introduction:

Asian Influence on Architecture and Design

Less is more. *Feng shui*. Zen sensibilities. We hear these terms tossed about, but what do they mean in our Western culture?

Today, as our society becomes increasingly diversified, more architects and designers incorporate elements of the Asian aesthetic and choose Eastern harmony over Victorian bric-a-brac. We see water elements and *shoji* screens as part of Western decor, traditional Asian materials such as bamboo and stone used more often, and amazing bathrooms that balance space indoors and out. Some architects adapt the Asian design philosophy of reducing a space to its core essentials to create a natural and simple minimalist look, ultimately adding a sense of serenity and tranquility.

Over the centuries, the Western interpretation of Asian design has ranged from conventional to contemporary. Nineteenth century Westerners perceived Asian countries as incredibly exotic — perhaps because they never thought they would visit them. Their arts were splendidly luxurious; their people had very different customs.

Since the travels of Marco Polo, the Chinese have established a tradition of trade with the West, but trading was sporadic until the sixteenth century, when the Portuguese opened up Canton in 1517 and Japan in 1542. By 1600, the British East India Company was founded, accelerating trade in the East. Subsequently, other trading companies (e.g., Dutch East Indies, French West, and East India Companies) joined them. From 1740 to 1870, Chinese cabinetmakers manufactured several types of furniture from Asian rose wood and bamboo for the Western market, including campaign chests, lap desks, trunks, and sea chests. Generally, the furniture was built in the Hepplewhite and Sheraton styles with several obvious Chinese changes such as dragon feet and other minor adaptations.

The European fascination with "the mysterious East" and its furniture and furnishings inspired the design of furniture and decorative arts throughout Western Europe. Lacquer from China and Japan, for instance, was responsible for the custom of "japanning" Western-made furniture during the early seventeen hundreds.

Westerners were particularly intrigued by the carvings of ivory, mother-of-pearl, tortoise shell, sandalwood, and hard stones. Asian designs of natural images added new layers of meaning. For example, cranes, which, because they live for many years, are thought to express life, are found in Japanese art. Chrysanthemums, which bloom late into the fall, are viewed as a symbol of long life. A traditional Chinese symbolic motif, such as the lotus, is the symbol of mental purity; the lotus grows in muddy waters yet itself is clean. Of course, of all motifs, the Chinese dragon is considered the most exotic.

Americans didn't enter the China trade until 1785 because British mercantile regulations had prevented the colonists from trading in Asia. Once the Treaty of Paris officially ended the American War for Independence in 1783, the Americans began to develop their own trade in China. The *Empress of China*, the first American merchant ship to reach China, arrived in Canton in 1784. Americans focused on goods such as porcelain, silks, and spices.

By 1840, Americans found Chinese export items less appealing and looked to Europeans to set the style for architecture, interior design, textile patterns, and fashion. When Commodore Perry and the U.S. Navy opened Japan to foreign trade in 1854, however, Americans were fascinated by its exotic and previously forbidden culture. Seafarers brought home porcelain vases, jade, lacquer, and carved teak wood. After the 1857 India

Mutiny, the British Empire took control of India. Suddenly, there was a great fascination in the East Indian culture. This interest died with the depression and ended with World War II.

By mid-twentieth century, many members of the American armed forces had been stationed in occupied Japan and later in Korea and Vietnam. They brought home their interest in Asian cultures, leading to increased export of Asian products. In the latter decades of the twentieth century, as many Westerners worked abroad and more Asians moved to the United States, interest grew in Asian styles such as seen in Burma, Indonesia, and Thailand in addition to those traditionally from China, India, and Japan. Westerners emulated the elegant lines and the simplicity of Asian architecture and design. Today, many Americans who have lived abroad incorporate their love for Asian design, their admiration for Asian concepts, and their Asian belongings in their decor here.

For example, the orientation of the house on the site and the use of natural materials such as bamboo flooring and granite counters often reflect Asian principles. Architects and designers have found the use of lightweight sliding screens, such as *shoji,* along with modern construction methods permit them to expand and extend the idea of multi-use interiors. To maintain the simplicity of the Asian design, some architects continue the beautiful wood ceilings and floor materials through the interior and exterior of the house. Another popular concept is *feng shui,* developed over three thousand years ago in China. This complex body of knowledge based on an understanding of nature is believed to help us balance the energies of any given space to ensure the inhabitants' good health and fortune. Over four thousand years old, this ancient Chinese art of placement allows the free flow of energy and guides our lives toward harmony.

Today, modern Western architects and designers are increasingly incorporating the best of the Asian aesthetic. They find that its beauty and simplicity, along with its rich cultural heritage, blend comfortably with other styles. Although this book is certainly not a complete encyclopedia of Asian architecture and design in the West, some beautiful examples can be found here.

Courtesy of D. Peter Lund

Conversations on Asian Design

Barney Maier

We recently designed a home with a *Zen* meditation room, another with a Chinese scholar-stone garden entry court, and yet another with a space for a Japanese soaking tub. How should we view these "Asian innovations"? Are they the latest fashion trend or something else? One might argue that borrowing design concepts from other cultures represents a search for something internal that one's own society may not provide. Certainly, elements of Asian design have appeared before now in America, but whether its presence then or now represents a yearning to find a missing ingredient is something about which we can only speculate. Indeed, the topic of Asian influences on American architectural design is complex and not well documented in the literature. It is a subject for scholarly inquiry, but that would not be appropriate for this book. What follows then is a contribution to the conversation prefaced by the ruminations of an architect with some awareness of the aesthetic interplay of East and West.

Asian design traditions have become part of the American scene. Some of America's most successful entrepreneurs, such as billionaires Larry Ellison of Oracle and Bill Gates of Microsoft have commissioned Asian-influenced homes designed by architects conversant with Japanese architecture. Asian (Japanese in particular) aesthetic ideas have influenced two of our foremost architects, Frank Lloyd Wright and Frank Gehry. Trend-setting *Dwell* magazine frequently features projects displaying Asian aesthetic influences. Mention *feng shui*[1] at a cocktail party, and chances are that people will nod in recognition.

Actually, the flow of ideas, aesthetic and otherwise, from abroad is an old story in the United States. Notwithstanding the frontier log cabin and sod house, traditional American home design came from European models and referenced European styles (e.g. Greek Revival, Gothic Revival, Italianate Victorian) that came to America along with European fashion. These styles migrated west across the North American continent. Elements of Asian design really start appearing during the Victorian era, a time of expansion and a period much enamored with the "exotic."

In the nineteenth century, Europeans and Americans referred to that vast area to the east of Europe as the "Orient" or the "East," which included cultures that range from Moorish to Indian to Chinese to Japanese. Victorian architecture is replete with Eastern influences, deriving from trade with these lands whose masterfully crafted items were in great demand. Along with imported porcelain settings, silk cloth, and Chinese court-inspired seating, Moorish-style turrets graced numerous Victorian dwellings. These oriental references—exotic trophies of expanded horizons—were appreciated as signs of our coming of age, becoming worldly and cosmopolitan. They were essentially gestures, conversation pieces.

The period of late Victorian to the present, like previous epochs, has witnessed paradigm shifts in design philosophy from Romantic to Rational[2]. Interestingly, one finds degrees of receptivity to Asian design at each end of the spectrum. In particular, Japanese design, much of which reflects Chinese origins, seems to have been an enduring resource. It has "romantic" appeal in its fashioning of contemplative spaces and idealized nature; it has "rational" appeal in its forthright use of materials and modular coherence.

At the end of the nineteenth century, the Arts and Crafts Movement flourished briefly (both in the U.S. and Europe). This movement, arising from a nostalgic sense of pre-industrial times, expressed disillusionment with the industrialized path society seemed headed down. Arts and Crafts homes featured straightforward expressions of joinery. Among the greatest practitioners of the art of joinery were the Japanese whose sublime aesthetic was undeniable to those who sought inspiration. The revered Gamble House in Pasadena, California, designed by architects Greene and Greene, clearly reflects this awareness and appreciation of the beauty of Japanese craft.

Then the work of Frank Lloyd Wright appeared. Well aware of Japanese design, he denied its influence on his work and indeed his homes could never be mistaken for their light airy dwellings. But the influence is undeniable: his open floor plan, the use of screens and panel detailing, fenestration, and, above all, the strong connection to nature. He called his work "organic" architecture: a building connected to the land was something the Japanese would surely appreciate.

The "modern" era of architectural design derives from the profound disillusionment that followed World War I. The Bauhaus architects of Germany and like-minded architects such as Le Corbusier practicing elsewhere in Europe formed the core of this movement. Philosophically, they rejected Beaux-Arts (Classical) composition as decadent and sought inspiration by going back to first principles. What is the nature of seat, of table, of shelter, of materials? The questions have a *Zen*-like quality in their exploration of the underlying "nature" of things. They can even be said to be very Japanese in seeking "honest" expression of materials. The Bauhaus credo *"Form follows Function"* opened the way to a more profound conversation with the East.

Modernism, also referred to as the International Style, swept America in the 1950s. Bauhaus philosophy informed the design of the corporate world, but this "style" was less readily accepted in the realm of residential design. The clear expression of solids and voids and general architectural composition challenged traditional images of "home." Nonetheless, notions of free-flowing space and a less formal living style gained ground in America as Wright's work and the derivative Ranch House took root.

Residential developments in California, where casual living is extolled, accelerated the changing perception of "home." California modern exemplified by the Eichler Homes[3], was influenced by both Bauhaus modernists (such as Miles van der Rohe, Richard Neutra, Walter Gropius) and by Frank Lloyd Wright. Homes featured low, sloped roofs, post and beam construction, and spaces that open onto nature. Spare form and planar composition characterized interior spaces. Spatially and structurally, they are vaguely reminiscent of traditional Japanese houses. They became an accepted part of the California landscape and their "cleansed" building form previewed the loosening of cultural givens.

Starting in the 1960, a period similar to the World War I period in its sense of alienation, the Hippie generation further challenged assumptions about traditional space and its underlying rationale. Buckminster Fuller domes, Yerts, and sod dwellings sprouted in various locations in "alternative America." This was a period —before consciousness of global warming and "Green Architecture"— of a re-evaluation of Humanity's relationship to Nature. Heralded by Rachel Carson's *Silent Spring* and nourished by the New Alchemists, Alan Watts' *The Way of Zen*, the *Whole Earth Catalog,* and other icons of the period, this "Boomer" generation sought to connect to nature and to reflect their values in aesthetic ways.

Thus, we arrive at twenty-first century America, whose hallmark is profound change and convergence. There is a new conversation between East and West: Asian influences on American architecture and design differ from the past in a significant way. The superiority of Western civilization is less taken for granted, and what constitutes "American" style is subject to wider interpretation. Receptivity to new aesthetics and concepts of space runs deeper than in the past.

Previously, Western house design, reflecting notions of security and formality, made a distinct separation between dwelling and environs: Man against the Wild (Nature) –not Man in Nature. "My house is my castle" conjures up the imagery of a citadel: inside is inside; outside is outside! Space is organized and separated into rooms, defined by function. You met guests in the Parlor, ate in the Dining Room, sipped cordials and smoked cigars in the Study, and so forth.

In contrast, in Japan and other parts of Asia, space flows more freely. Usage of "rooms" often relates more to circumstances than formal assignment. Traditionally, Japanese define spaces by location: "inner" space and "outer" space, there being no specific equivalent for the word "room." A given space may be used during the day as living space and, at night, as sleeping space. Using post and beam construction with sliding partitions, spaces could be reconfigured and enlarged: the interior world could readily be integrated into the outside world (nature). Another way of thinking about the difference between a traditional American home and a traditional Japanese home is this: a Japanese house is more an extension of the context (site) that it is in; an American house is more an object in that context.

These differences result from our different ways of perceiving the environment. China and Japan (Korea, Thailand, Vietnam, etc.) share "Eastern" values in a broad sense: common to them is the historic imprint of Buddhism (Taoism and Confucianism[4]). Unlike the desert-born religions Judaism, Islam, and Christianity, which set Man apart, Buddhism and Taoism strongly connect Man to Nature. As exemplified by *feng shui*, what connects is more in focus than what divides. Spaces and energies flow and impact on each other.

Sympathetic parallel developments allow for convergence. Although its aesthetic underpinning derives from different sources, the iconic Philip Johnson glass house in New Canaan, Connecticut, could have been built in Japan. Featuring glass walls sandwiched between roof and floor planes, the building establishes the primacy of symbol and ritual in spatial terms that is, indeed, more Japanese Tea Ceremony space than American Living Room. Do such spaces fit our life style?

Perhaps... The Loft Space, the new paragon of sophistication, has strong appeal because its space can be variously configured and released from the confinement of rooms: a strong market for *shoji* screens! Those who can, increasingly bring gardens into their homes as domains of serenity. Bathrooms have soaking tubs. There are quiet, uncluttered spaces for meditation.

Whether we are aware or not, Asian models can provide templates for new ways of inhabiting the spaces we create. Bringing these concepts into our buildings can enrich our lives. As the twenty-first century unfolds and our world becomes smaller, we expect to see more fusion between Eastern and Western styles. What follows are fine examples of a new phase in the conversation between Asia and America.

Formerly a principal in his own Connecticut architectural firm, Maier and Giannelli, Barney relocated to Massachusetts in 1997, where he worked for various Boston area firms. In 2001, he joined Feinmann, Inc., where his design expertise and insight have contributed to many award-winning residential designs.

Barney earned a degree in Chinese Studies from Middlebury College and holds a Masters of Architecture from UCLA, where his thesis advisor was the late Charles Moore. He currently resides with his wife and son in Arlington, Massachusetts.

[1]"Feng" means "wind" and "shui" means "water" (pronounced fung-shway). It is based on the Taoist vision and understanding of nature, particularly on the idea that the land is alive and filled with Chi, or energy. Wind and water must flow freely without obstruction. Thus in general practice, *feng shui* is about the proper harmonizing of (built) elements on a site.

[2]"Romantic" exemplified by Art Deco, Arts and Crafts and "Rational" exemplified by Bauhaus/International Style and Green Architecture.

[3]Joseph Eichler (1900 - 1974) was one of the nation's most influential builders of modern homes. California-based, his post-war residential real estate developments were known for their innovative Modernist style. Between 1950 and 1974, his company, Eichler Homes, built over 11,000 homes in Northern California, three communities in Southern California and locations back east. Known as Eichlers, they changed the California lifestyle. (Based on excerpt from Wikipedia)

[4]The impact of Confucianism on Asian cultures relates more to the conservative longevity of traditional architectural forms than to a philosophy of the continuity of living things.

2.

Building in an Asian Style

Asian influence on architecture can often be seen in the movement from the public areas of the house to the more private areas. In Chinese and Mogul architecture, buildings often enclose open space and lead from one courtyard to another. Think of the Imperial Palace in Beijing, China. Symmetry and balance between the parts of a building are stressed.

Generally, Western architecture emphasizes height, while Asian architecture emphasizes the horizontal axis and bilateral symmetry. As in Greek architecture, the framing is almost exclusively a system of uprights and horizontals, and little use is made of diagonal members. The columns, rafters, and the great overhanging roofs contribute vitality and grace. An upper class Japanese dwelling is noteworthy for its refinement and simplicity. Interior posts form a supporting skeleton for the roof. The exterior walls usually consist of movable panels that slide in grooves.

Photography by James Abts, Hamilton, Massachusetts

Vermont Japanese Temple

Like traditional Japanese gates, the building sits up on wood piers that lead to the entrance of the building. The forms and palette of the materials are rooted in the local vernacular of shingle style, so the building feels comfortable and familiar. Yet the treatment of the window walls and the clean lines of the masonry are contemporary, allowing the owner a wonderful experience of transparency—of being aware of the changing mood of the day. *Courtesy of Jim Westphalen*

TruexCullins designed this home, which sits amidst the beauty of the natural world in the hills above Lake Champlain, Vermont. The project goals were that the home should be made of natural materials, be integrated into the surrounding landscape, and give the owners a sense of joy and spiritual sustenance. The roof extends out over the porch, which serves to connect the inside with the glorious outside. *Courtesy of Jim Westphalen*

The exposed exterior materials are naturally weathering cedar, copper, and stone. No preservatives were used, which will let the building age gracefully and grow more beautiful over time. *Courtesy of Jim Westphalen*

The home is nestled into the west facing hills above the lake, so that the visitor does not see the structure until approaching it. In this way, it is respectful of the surrounding landscape and preserves the views of the Adirondack Mountains for those neighbors further up the hill. This nestling also gives the owners and their young children a wonderful sense of arrival and refuge. *Courtesy of Jim Westphalen*

Much of the structure is left exposed and is understood as the joints and bones of the building. In places, the structure is carried from the inside to the outside, reinforcing the notion that the home is part of the surrounding environment and is a refuge from the busy work life of the client. *Courtesy of Jim Westphalen*

Palladio Hill House

The approach is a controlled procession: the limestone-walled walkway brings visitors to the monumental entry gate and the footbridge that enters the upper level of the home. Although many small windows are on the street facade of the house, the few large windows do not provide direct views into the primary living spaces. At the custom-built front door, the visitor is not given a hint of the spaces to come or of the valley view beyond. © *Paul Bardagjy*

The client wished to present a quiet face to the street while having tranquil, yet dynamic and unusual spaces within. Studio H & L designed a residence with a recurring balance between opposites such as the curving and circular walls playing against the straight lines of other walls and the details of doors and windows. *Feng shui* principles provided guidance for the placement of the 5,500 square foot house on the site and supported the relationships and orientation of the spaces within. The massing, footprint, and roof line with its deep eaves are simple and rectangular, giving the home a horizontal emphasis despite its two-story height. The exterior materials are deliberately subtle and muted. © *Paul Bardagjy*

Inside the entry foyer on the upper floor, the house opens in front of the guest. The open living room and dining room are to either side. Sliding exterior doors offer access to decks and views north toward the valley, the ceiling rises overhead with clerestory windows adding to the illumination, and an undulating wall, which gives shape to all the living spaces, encircles the kitchen and its wall of windows. In the living room, the curved wall is repeated in a *shoji*-like screen wall, where traditional rice paper is updated and interpreted in laminated glass. Studio H & L also designed the steel-and-stone coffee and side tables for the living room. These tables have tops of solid granite and loose river rock. The interior colors are natural with emphasis on warm wood accents, gold and parchment colors for the walls and floors, and contrasting darker wood shades for cabinets and in furniture finishes. © *Paul Bardagjy*

At the other end of the winding wall is the nearly circular kitchen. © *Paul Bardagjy*

The powder room is explicitly naturalistic. Its counter appears to be carved from a block of granite, and the mirror inserted into what seems to be a rough-hewn cross section of a tree. Even the flooring of pebbles looks to have been worn smooth by flowing waters. © *Paul Bardagjy*

The circle is considered favorable and fortunate in Asian design. The kitchen has a faceted wall of windows enclosing custom cabinetry. The large, half-round island is intended not only as a dining area but also as a theater for cooking classes. The exhaust hood above the island was designed for the house and built by a local stainless fabricator. At nearly 90 inches long, it spans over several, commercial-style cooking appliances. © *Paul Bardagjy*

The master bath shows the special status often given to these private spaces. The travertine walls and floors continue into the large sunken shower and bath. This bathing area is minimally detailed with its edge defined only by the steps down. Floating in the room is a round, custom lavatory cabinet with its eye-catching *yin yang* granite counter, vessel sinks, and cable-supported mirror and lights. The *yin yang* countertop in the master bathroom is an overt use of Asian symbolism to glorify this important space. © *Paul Bardagjy*

The striking circular space of the kitchen is repeated downstairs as the bedroom of the master suite. The suite is entered through a sitting room open to the bedroom. The windows have automated window coverings that open the room to the natural surroundings at the touch of a button. Studio H + L designed the platform bed and side tables specifically for this bedroom. © *Paul Bardagjy*

Virginian Engawa

Carter + Burton Architecture designed this Virginia home (built by Jon Duval) to stretch out along the east-west axis, taking advantage of passive solar strategies on the southern elevation and the panoramic views to the valley. The slope of the modified shed roof relates to the surrounding natural area: low horizontal lines mimic the plane of the grasses, and the edge of the higher shed roof is aligned with the existing tree line. The exterior materials of stucco, timber, and copper create a low maintenance, regional response to the surrounding agrarian setting. *Courtesy of Jim Burton*

Highlighting the client's interest in Japanese architecture, the "solar *engawa*" serves as a connection piece in multiple ways. *Engawa* describes space that is both inside and outside. Here, the walls separating the interior from the exterior of the house are glass, so the inside hallway blends with the outside terrace and views of the Blue Ridge Mountains beyond. The cantilevered shading louvers provide solar protection in the summer months and bring the scale down at the *engawa* layer. *Courtesy of Daniel Azfal*

The open risers of this locally crafted stair tower at the core of the house link views through spaces both vertically and horizontally while allowing natural light to pass through all the way down to the basement. The open stairs provide flexibility, light, ventilation, and the appearance of extra space. The concrete floor from the living room hallway wraps around the corner of the core. *Courtesy of Daniel Azfal*

This modern country kitchen emphasizes family connection. The built-in benches in the corner provide an informal breakfast area with game and blanket storage under the seating. The passive solar design placed all of the cabinets below the countertop using dish drawers for storage below. The large overhangs warm the countertops in the winter and shade them in the summer. The pantry core creates a shift in the circulation axis and provides ample storage including a butler's pantry, connecting the kitchen to the formal dining space. High north windows above the pantry provide balanced daylighting, and the wood ceiling provides warmth while bringing the scale of the space down for a more cozy setting. *Courtesy of Daniel Azfal*

Westport Meadow House

Designed by Maryann Thompson Architects, this one-story house nestles into a forty-acre meadow along the Westport River. Surrounded by stone walls, the river, and a veil of trees along the river's edge, the site reads in a series of striated layers, both horizontally along the ground plane and vertically between the meadow and the sky. The roof planes and the expansive decks extend into the landscape, accentuating the overall horizontality of the house. Program elements are appropriately distributed across this threshold according to the daily path of the sun. © *Chuck Choi Architectural Photography*

Eighteen hundred square feet of deck surface stretch along the western and southern elevations. Along the western elevation, floor and ceiling planes negotiate the threshold between interior and exterior, allowing the landscape to bleed into the house and extending the interior living spaces outside. The deck perforates the plan at the entry, creating a modified "dog trot" condition. Enclosed on either side by the living room and master bedroom, this dogtrot space reads an "interiorized" outdoor room and a threshold between public and private spaces. Sliding doors at the corners in the living room and master bedroom open to non-axial views of the site, while drawing light and cross-ventilation deep into the body of the scheme. When the doors are fully open these interior spaces serve as screened porches. Deep roof overhangs borrowed from Asian temple architecture provide the shelter and enclosure of indoor spaces with orientation and connection to the outdoors. © *Chuck Choi Architectural Photography*

A wood-clad "organizing wall" skewers the scheme, alternately revealing and concealing both interior and exterior views. Embedded in the house, the organizing wall's "exteriorized" skin renders ambiguous the boundary between inside and outside, throwing the program spaces that line the east and west facades to the outdoors. © *Chuck Choi Architectural Photography*

Hovering just above the ground and oriented axially along a gentle slope of the meadow, the house is a continuation of the landscape condition, echoing the layered and horizontal nature of the site. © *Chuck Choi Architectural Photography*

The exposed structure recalls Japanese architectural traditions, where posts and beams take the roof loads and walls are diaphanous and mutable *shoji* screens. Here, the skin is light and operable, allowing it to shift, mutate, and get out of the way. © *Chuck Choi Architectural Photography*

Sliding doors, which open at the corners of the living room, "break the box" and allow for a dynamic reading of the architecture and a shifting edge between inside and outside. Light through the four-sided clerestory in the living room illuminates the volume with changing patterns throughout the day and across the seasons. © *Chuck Choi Architectural Photography*

Like the teahouses of Japanese strolling gardens, the Westport Meadow House is essentially a roofed pavilion that both joins and separates the meadow and river, while providing a vantage from which to take in the landscape. © *Chuck Choi Architectural Photography*

Bali High

The house has a pagoda roof with five courses of cedar shingles as a starter course to give a cope at the edge. The moon gate opens to the inner courtyard with its koi pond and walled garden water trough, which continues around to the pond below and is pumped back to the other side of the house — reminiscent of the Chinese water architecture gardens. *Photography by James Abts, Hamilton, Massachusetts*

A lily pond surrounds this Balinese style house designed by Connecticut's Jonathan Isleib. It sits on a 160-foot cliff overlooking the harbor and the river. The circular moon window affords an intimate view of the cloistered Japanese garden on the other side of the ledge. The copper clad garden enclosure with the round top resembles those in Thailand. *Photography by James Abts, Hamilton, Massachusetts*

Both the living room Balinese pavilion and the dining/kitchen building have copper clad finals. Walking stones through the garden allow traffic from the main terrace left to the dining room (right) up the steps. The glass, at left, slides completely into the wall behind the stonework. *Photography by James Abts, Hamilton, Massachusetts*

This hall connects the foyer to the dining/family/kitchen areas. It has curly maple floors and a two-sided fireplace. An Imari platter hangs above. *Photography by James Abts, Hamilton, Massachusetts*

This interior garden has a custom hip-roofed skylight with native granite walls and site-found lichen boulders. The watering system at the base of the skylight maintains the fern and moss garden. The Asian mask on the left acts as a guardrail for ascending to the main floor. Indian slate borders grey green tiles in a staggered bond pattern. *Photography by James Abts, Hamilton, Massachusetts*

The lower level office area has a collection of Japanese dance masks and love seats made from Asian sea grass. The grey green tile floor coordinates with the lichen-colored rock in the interior and exterior. *Photography by James Abts, Hamilton, Massachusetts*

The client was in the Asian tour business. Their collection seen in this living room includes Balinese, Indian, African, and Polynesian pieces. On the far wall is a Japanese coromandel screen. The white cedar walls contrast with the red cedar pagoda ceiling and the French limestone floor with bluestone border. All the windows/doors slide behind the walls for a true Balinese pavilion style impervious to the weather. The five-foot overhangs shelter the room from brilliant sun. *Photography by James Abts, Hamilton, Massachusetts*

Breeze House

Entering the Breeze House, designed by Glen Ireni, can be likened to walking through a garden gate. One never feels that the outdoor environment of this coastal neighborhood is ever left behind. The front view of the house expresses the same modest scale of its neighborhood and the playfulness that lies deeper within. *Courtesy of Derek Rath*

This child's bedroom illustrates the use of natural light and the large *shoji* screen sliders that open onto the indoor/outdoor breezeway that flanks the swimming pool. *Courtesy of Derek Rath*

The community pavilion enjoys natural daylight that streams through voids between the lofty roof plane and the "screen walls." The celestial lighting arrangement reflects off glass in all directions recalling the night sky during evening gatherings. During the day, it gazes over the serene private garden and pool. By maintaining the entire program on a single, 3,000 square-foot floor plate, all the living spaces, including circulation areas, intimately engage the garden, natural light, and ocean air. The living spaces wrap around an 85-foot long swimming pool "mote" and garden. *Courtesy of Derek Rath*

The master bedroom pavilion enjoys more shelter and privacy than other spaces in the house. *Courtesy of Derek Rath*

The master bathroom vanity overlooks a secluded sculpture courtyard and enjoys ample morning sunlight. *Courtesy of Derek Rath*

The large glass panel to the left of the pool opens to the private pavilion's breezeway that connects all the bedrooms with the garden. *Courtesy of Derek Rath*

This view from the private garden reveals the light, soaring forms of the roofs and the connection between the community, private and guest "pavilions" as well as their connections with the garden. Glen Ireni conceived the roof planes as organic, strengthening the inhabitants' engagement with nature. *Courtesy of Derek Rath*

A dynamic view of the pool greets every visitor at the entry and instantly expresses the home's relationship to the garden and the clarity of the plan. *Courtesy of Derek Rath*

Japanese Concepts of Space

Hays+Ewing Design Studio designed this 2,500 square-foot, ecologically intelligent house for their use. Located in Charlottesville, Virginia, the house draws inspiration from houses in Japan and Europe, where they both lived and studied. There are numerous green strategies at work in the house: some influence the well being of the family members; others positively affect their health; and still others contribute to the health of the environment. © *Prakash Patel*

The house is split in two parts with a bridge spanning over the entry court. The bridge is a place of transition and connectivity, both joining and separating the public and private spaces within the house while expanding the boundaries of the interior to the outdoors. From the entry, the bridge and flanking structure frame a view of the landscape. © *Prakash Patel*

Two Japanese concepts of space provided the conceptual framework for the design of the house. The first, known as *ma*, refers to the spatial interval between two objects or two edges. The second, *hashi*, refers to bridging the two edges. These edges can be either physical, like chopsticks bridging between the plate and the mouth, or symbolic, spanning between the secular world and the heavenly world. Located in an old mill village, this house is itself a place between; it feels both urbane (little more than a mile from downtown) and pastoral (the flood plains deter high-density development); it acts as the bridge spanning between the urbane and pastoral, public and private. © *Prakash Patel*

Architects often confront competing goals in projects. Hays + Ewing oriented the house parallel to the street grid and created a house that fit well in the neighborhood. © *Prakash Patel*

Embodying the Japanese spatial concepts of *ma,* or a spatial/temporal distance—the space between that is not nothingness—and *hashi*, or bridging two edges, the glazed bridge serves as a sitting room and connects the public/family spaces to the private master bedroom. A transition zone, it makes a strong connection to the outdoors. It is fully glazed on the two view walls creating a quality of suspension. The other two walls are painted to match the adjacent exterior siding to reinforce the interpenetration of landscape and house. © *Philip Beaurline*

The kitchen has the best field of vision anywhere in the house. This vision also encompasses the much used deck and the outdoor play area. Many details were employed to enhance the potential for family interaction. For example, a bar seating area is located on the other side of the kitchen island, providing opportunity for the children and parents to spend time together even while cooking and doing homework. The fiber cement flooring, stained a similar color as the deck, visually connects the indoors to the outdoors. © *Prakash Patel*

In the master bath, identical translucent glass doors flank the vanity, one leading to a separate toilet, the other to a shower. To hide a potentially unsightly return duct vent, a custom slatted wood door flanks one side of the sink. An identical door flanks the other side of the vanity and hides the medicine cabinet. © *Prakash Patel*

Creating a dialogue and harmony between architecture and landscape is fundamental in Asian design. Here, the architects collaborated with Nelson Byrd Woltz Landscape Architects, who selected native species for the gardens, resulting in a design that fits well in the Virginia setting. Naturally acclimated to the climate, the plants require little or no irrigation and won't adversely affect the habitat, as can non-indigenous species. © *Philip Beaurline*

The street grid is 28 degrees off south, resulting in primary house views facing south-southwest, a condition that could compromise the passive solar optimization. Consequently, the architects integrated louvers and trellises to provide shading in the summer while allowing the warming light to penetrate the house in the winter. © *Philip Beaurline*

"Texas Zen" House

The "Texas Zen" house designed by Webber+Studio incorporates three pavilions unified by a large roof creating Asian-influenced regionalism. The first pavilion holding the house's main public functions is almost separated from the main body of the house. The two private pavilions contain the master suite and children's rooms. Each of these slip between existing mature trees on the site. One is raised up at the back of the house to allow for a covered porch below. The big roof that unifies the pavilions recalls rural Texas gambrels and is punctuated by dormers that moderate the scale in interior spaces. The resulting mass is much understated on the street in spite of its size and context. The use of Texas limestone, river rock, oak millwork, and mahogany accent woods lends the house a Balinese air while referring to local context. Expansive decks and terraces achieved the owner's desire for indoor-outdoor living. *Courtesy of mcconnellphoto.net ©2008*

The knife edge eaves detail with birch plywood soffit allows morning light to flow into the public pavilion and entry pergola. *Courtesy of mcconnellphoto.net ©2008*

The entry pergola is constructed from steel and redwood. Local Texas limestone tile leads to the custom steel-clad front door and into the public spaces beyond. *Courtesy of mcconnellphoto.net ©2008*

Floor to ceiling windows flood the public pavilion space with natural light during the day. The corner pivot doors open to the entry pergola for entertaining and catching breezes. *Courtesy of mcconnellphoto.net ©2008*

Limestone tile from local sources continue inside the house from the pergola. The dining area is located under a mahogany paneled box for intimacy within the public pavilion. The dining room light fixture is a paper lantern. *Courtesy of mcconnellphoto.net ©2008*

Hand finished limestone countertops and rift sawn white oak millwork are used throughout the kitchen. The counter terminates in a box that houses the kitchen pantry and storage area. *Courtesy of mcconnellphoto.net ©2008*

The family room is open to the children's play area above. The translucent glass panels evoke *shoji* screens. The entertainment center also contains storage space and bookcases in the stairway behind. *Courtesy of mcconnellphoto.net ©2008*

The guest bedroom looks out to the front garden area. The floor is ipe. *Courtesy of mcconnellphoto.net ©2008*

Exposed structural beams and the ipe floors flow out to the covered porch beyond. Sliding floor-to-ceiling steel door panels separate the family room from the office. *Courtesy of mcconnellphoto.net ©2008*

The master bath has a mahogany bath surround and countertops along with Texas limestone tiled floor and walls. The windows open to the garden beyond. *Courtesy of mcconnellphoto.net ©2008*

The guest bath has a river rock tiled shower, limestone floor, and mesquite countertop. The built in bench adds additional storage space. *Courtesy of mcconnellphoto.net ©2008*

The rear terrace at dusk with the family room beyond. The exposed structural beams flow out from the family room. Ipe-boxed tube steel supports the bedroom above. *Courtesy of mcconnellphoto.net ©2008*

California Sushi

Architect David Wright designed this 4,400 square-foot modern adaptation of Japanese style in the Sierra Nevada mountains of California. The house, which uses SIPs, is much like the traditional Japanese *tatami* (straw mat) module. *Courtesy of Steve Solinsky*

The traditional clay Japanese roof tiles provide natural cooling and aesthetics. The design, which merges the exterior with the interior, creates a number of micro-climate zones: sun and shade porches, screened porch room, basement cool zones, and passive solar great room. *Courtesy of Steve Solinsky*

Native wood, such as locally produced Douglas fir, cedar and pine lumber, is used throughout. *Courtesy of Steve Solinsky*

The radiant heated concrete floors are surfaced with native granite. They provide solar thermal mass and efficient heat distribution throughout the house. *Courtesy of Steve Solinsky*

To maintain the simplicity of the Asian design, Wright continued the beautiful wood ceilings and floor materials through the interior. Ceilings fans keep the interior air flowing in both summer and winter. *Courtesy of Steve Solinsky*

The south-facing glass and high venting skylights bring the magnificent scenery into the house. *Courtesy of Steve Solinsky*

Red Oak Retreat Home

A meandering drive in the mountains of Woodville, Virginia, brings you to this hidden paradise of secluded valleys and stream crossings. Large rock outcroppings to the south help inspire the use of stone, both inside and outside, this eastern-inspired retreat home designed by Carter Burton. As the roof line rises, rooms step down from the front of the house to the back, achieving a theater effect oriented towards the valley and the mountains in the distance. *Courtesy of Daniel Azfal*

The south angle of this residence fans towards the sun to create an ideal east-west access. Touching the earth lightly, a ground-faced concrete block pier system captures the panoramic view. Many of the public spaces, including the great room, the kitchen, and the sun room, are massed in this rear southern section. *Courtesy of Daniel Azfal*

The clients insisted upon the use of natural materials—stone tile, wood, and glass—throughout the entire home. With the help of sculptor Richard Lew, the owner crafted all tile and stone flooring, granite countertops, and exterior stonewalls and terraces. The final design is a fairly compact plan that uses materials, light, and views to connect with the natural surroundings. *Courtesy of Daniel Azfal*

River rock surrounds the house, anchoring it with the natural rock outcroppings. The owner, a landscape designer, had the house designed to work with his ideas of terracing the site. Each room directly accesses the terraces across the concrete bridges spanning over the river rock trench drain. *Courtesy of Daniel Azfal*

This corner window resolves the intersection of all the project elements in a poetic way. The concrete subsill and cantilevered timbers allow the window mullions to line up around the house in spite of the stepping complexities. The custom stainless rain chain allows for a gentle stream of water from the large roof to wash over the river rock surrounding the house. *Courtesy of Daniel Azfal*

Horizontal elements such as window mullions, exterior wood siding, and horizontally struck concrete block contribute to this home's *Zen* sensibilities. The warm and intimate interior spaces that contrast to the expansive surroundings outside reinforce its human scale. There is a strong inside to outside relationship on the south terraces. *Courtesy of Daniel Azfal*

The custom cedar windows by Bergerson feature a small integrated operable unit in each frame. *Courtesy of Daniel Azfal*

The wood timber framing has an eastern feel and logic while the compact house shape reflects mountaintop retreats in the Shenandoah Valley region. Evoking the clouds outside, the floating light fixture defines a space within the space. *Courtesy of Daniel Azfal*

The kitchen is designed as a wooden box/stage, where the couple can enjoy cooking and still visit with guests. Placing the kitchen in a central location is ideal in the nine-part grid that is often seen in *feng shui* design. Four columns, structural beams, and suspended cabinets delineate the space and accentuate its role as the heart of the house. A custom maple cabinet separates the kitchen from the lower living space, providing integrated storage for the home entertainment system. The house features an energy-efficient geothermal mechanical system, strong SIPs in the roof, and a cistern to provide water for plants. *Courtesy of Daniel Azfal*

Modern Japanese Castle

Designed by Robert Oshatz and constructed in Obihiro, Japan, this residence bridges the aesthetics of two disparate cultures; emblematic of neither, yet summoning echoes of both. Built to accommodate the busy lifestyle of the president of one of Hokkaido's major construction firms and to provide a place of repose for his parents, the house was conceived to appear as a radiant jewel in the midst of an urban garden oasis. The internal spaces are articulated by the use of straight and curving glue laminated Douglas fir beams. On the upper level, beams are wrapped on a tight radius to create a portal-type circulation corridor that runs as a spine along the building and provides access to the more private areas. On the lower level, they are used to provide a pleasing sense of movement throughout the spaces. The radial arrangement of the plan helps to unify the building visually, as well as bracing it against earthquake tremors. In referring to his house, the client said, "This house makes me very happy; it speaks to me." *Courtesy of Yoshihiko Tobari*

The front gate and the western red privacy fence that runs along the perimeter of the property, as seen from the street. *Courtesy of Yoshihiko Tobari*

A view from the second floor roof deck showing the exterior door of the sitting room. *Courtesy of Yoshihiko Tobari*

A view of the service entrance with the large stainless steel family crest in the foreground. *Courtesy of Yoshihiko Tobari*

The focal point of the first floor is the sunken conversation pit, featuring a fireplace and a built-in sofa. The double-height ceiling maintains a spatial connection to private spaces above. *Courtesy of Yoshihiko Tobari*

The right side of the gallery provides a series of alcoves that are used to display artwork. *Courtesy of Yoshihiko Tobari*

California Contemporary Japanese Style Home

In this project, the owner worked with Remodel West to design and build a home that was influenced by Japanese architecture and materials. Vertical grain Douglas fir, which is traditionally used in Japanese architecture, was selected for the cabinetry, ceiling trim, and baseboards, and within the *tatami* room in the background. Quarter sawn red oak flooring, which was used on the floor throughout the house, features a very hard straight grain complimenting the straight grain of the Douglas fir. *Courtesy of Mert Carpenter Photography*

Early on in the project, Remodel West designed a *tatami* room, which allowed a precise fitting of *tatami* mats. A local Japanese carpenter was commissioned to assist to build the *shoji* screens. The design and construction firm responsible for building the home coordinated the installation of built-in track systems, which allow a simple and clean appearance for the screens. The *tokonomo* (a display alcove) features a hardwood material sliced from a log with bark intact and a furniture piece. The middle mat lifts up and reveals a hidden foot well for western style dining. *Courtesy of Mert Carpenter Photography*

This contemporary style kitchen has heavy Asian influences with its use of vertical grain Douglas fir. The horizontal and vertical window elements introduce natural light while blocking an uninteresting view. A custom-designed *shoji* style cabinet in the kitchen coordinates with other *shoji* details, maintaining continuity. *Courtesy of Mert Carpenter Photography*

The kitchen is open to the adjacent family room. The custom *shoji* screen panels conceal unique horizontal window detail. Recessed vaulted ceiling detail brings in more natural light while introducing a more contemporary element for California style desires. *Courtesy of Mert Carpenter Photography*

In this view of living and dining room, you can see that the exterior is introduced in a balanced manner. Antique furniture pieces blend old world tradition with contemporary elements. *Courtesy of Mert Carpenter Photography*

This family room has an asymmetrical design, which is common in Japanese architecture. The cabinet conceals the audio video components. To the right of the flat screen TV is a vertical window, which introduces a "peek-a-boo" view of the back yard. *Courtesy of Mert Carpenter Photography*

This built-in desk area, which coordinates with the architecture and materials of the home, offers a practical solution for a busy California lifestyle. Recessed vaulted ceiling detail in the office nook includes operable skylights with built-in blinds. The flooring is quarter sawn red oak. The sliding pocket doors were designed and built to compliment the *shoji* screens visible from the nook. *Courtesy of Mert Carpenter Photography*

The master bath features a deep Japanese style soaking tub. Material choices were intended to provide a soothing experience while bathing. *Courtesy of Mert Carpenter Photography*

This powder room, tucked around the corner from the kitchen, provides a new experience from the public area of the home. Slate tiles and a chiseled granite vessel style sink bring warmth and Asian influence to this contemporary California home. *Courtesy of Mert Carpenter Photography*

Colorado Minka

While living in Japan, the owners found an 1831 folk house or *minka*, which they disassembled and moved to Colorado to form the basis for a new house that would incorporate Japanese design concepts. To ensure spaces created inside the house would enhance and accept structures from the Japanese *minka*, the owners worked closely with their architects, Clyde Reynolds Carpenter, FAIA, Professor, School of Architecture, University of Kentucky, and Clay Lancaster Endowed Professor and Chair, Historic Preservation, College of Design, and Scott Guyon, AIA, both of Lexington, Kentucky. They designed the house to capture the outdoors and essence of Japanese style both inside and outside. The concepts of Japanese design which are based on *wabi* (simple and quiet) and *sabi* (elegant simplicity, a perception of beauty, and a closeness with nature) were instrumental in shaping the final design. Roof lines captured the lines of Japanese temple (*jiin*) or house, which incorporated *iri-moya* or hipped gabled roof line. The five rounded dormers were the architect's interpretation of the helmet-styled dormers of a Japanese *minka.* The pavilion at the left resembles a small temple. *Photo by Rod Hanna*

This view shows the east end of the house and pavilion at the west end of house. Windows at the east end are in the master bath. The doorway leads into a north side hallway (*hiro-en -engawa*). Exterior walls or *kabe* were stucco (Sto product) to simulate earthen walls of a *minka*. Pebble areas and flagstone (*shiki-ishi*) pathways surround the house, imitating Japanese *Zen* (raked sand) gardens. Granite slabs, which serve as steps to decks and bridges over the stream, were once curbstones in Baltimore that were quarried in the late 1800s. Rock gardens with wildflowers, evergreens, deciduous trees, and shrubs grace the hillside behind house. Most rocks/boulders were native to property. *Photo by Rod Hanna*

This view of the side yard actually shows the front entrance behind the aspens. Because bamboo would not survive in the winter climate, the owners planted aspen trees closely to provide a sense of tranquility. When mature, their trunks will approximate a mature bamboo grove. The flagstone pathway leads from entrance gate (*mon*) to the front door steps and deck. Rock-lined stream (*ogawa*) flows under the hallway bridge (*hashi*) to the pavilion and down through the side yard to a pond for recirculation to a waterfall viewed from the kitchen and master bedroom. Transom windows above the doors and windows capture more of the exterior views. *Photo by Rod Hanna*

Shakkei is an architectural concept using scenery as background in design, which was easily accomplished here, given the spectacular, seventeen-acre setting. Incidentally, the master bow maker for the Emperor of Japan blessed the site before construction. The house was south facing and ran east-west along the south sloping hillside. The main entrance was on the west side or side of joy and pleasure. Long hallways running the full length of the house along both north and south sides provide access to the functional rooms located between the hallways. Exterior doorways lined the hallways to bring the outside inside. The use of *oku* or the concept of feeling of distance while looking through doorways or windows to other rooms or gardens was also applied. Care was taken to blend the old and new. The gate in the foreground is a replica of a Japanese gate made from minka beams (*bari*) and new Japanese roof tiles (*oni-gawara*). *Photo by Rod Hanna*

Normally, the entry or *genkan* would have a dirt floor as it is still considered outside of house. Here, visitors and family members take off their shoes and slip on interior slippers keeping the dirt outside. Sliding wooden doors provide storage for exteriorly worn shoes (*kutsu*) or clogs/sandals (*geta*). The wooden step with sliding doors is called a shoebox or *geta hako* or *kutsu hako* and is from the *minka*. On top of the *geta-hako* are two pairs of *geta*, a black metal temple lantern or *toro*, and an early American designed wrought iron candle lamp/holder. The stone step is a late 1800s granite curbstone from Baltimore, Maryland. The *shoji* doors on the left are called *yuki-mi-shoji* or snow viewing *shoji* because the small panels in middle of door have glass behind them allowing one to slide the panels open to view outside. A coat closet is located behind this pair of *shojis*. Hanging on right wall is a five-panel *noren, a* hand painted waterfall (*taki*) scene in traditional blue and white. *Norens* are generally found hanging in doorways of shops or restaurants. Below the *noren* on the floor is a long wooden mallet or rice mortar used to pound rice for rice cakes (*mochi*). The two large glass and wood sliding doors were the front doors of *minka* and are called *genkan-iriguchi*. Beyond these doors lies the dining room and *hiro-en-engawa* or north side interior veranda or hallway. To the left of these doors, is a wooden carved fish that serves as a door bell (*kane*). Striking the fish with a mallet produces the sound. Down the *hiro-en-engawa* on the right is a contemporary Karen Young wood block print of kimonos. Further down is a formal black silk Japanese *kimono* worn by married women. The wooden floor boards (*age-ita*) of the *hiro-en-engawa* are pine (*matsu*) from the *minka*. *Photo by Rod Hanna*

The sliding doors to the left are the front doors (*genkan-iriguchi*) from the *minka*. The hanging carving above doors is a *ranma*. The Late Edo era (1603-1867 A.D.) six-panel folding Japanese screen or *byobu* on the wall depicts a single pine (*matsu*) tree held in place by a pair of chrome/brass duck *byobu* holders (one at lower right). Above the *byobu* is a beam (*bari*) from *minka* to frame *byobu*. Waviness adds interest. Also at the right end of *byobu* is a small tea ceremony box. To the right of table is the *tokonoma* or recessed area, where flowers and prized family items are displayed. The traditional meditation alcove, *Tokonoma,* is framed by two posts (*hashira*) from *minka*: one sooted and one unsooted. The shelf is from a large walnut (*kurumi*) tree from New Jersey and top is a burled aspen (*hakoyanagi*) log from Colorado, representing the last three locations where the owners lived. The elderly father of a close Malaysian friend of the owner painted the hanging scroll (*kakejiki*). The black woven basket on *tokonoma* is used for *ikebana* flower arrangement. A *kutani* vase with flowers adorns the opposite end of shelf. An oriental design rug under the table was hand tied in China. A North Carolina furniture maker made the cherry dining room table; Thonet bentwood and cane chairs are by Stendig. A Nagoya style *obi* serves as table runner with a red lacquer Vietnamese bamboo plate in center. *Photo by Rod Hanna*

The great room or *ima* has 14-foot ceilings (*tenjo*) to allow enough height for two-level beam structure. Sooted posts (*joya-habira*) support multi-level *matsu* sooted beams, including *chona-bari* or cross beams and *ushi-bari* or longitudinal beams. Curved beams were used in *minkas* as they were stronger than straight members. Posts and beams were sooted from smoke from *iroris* or sunken open hearths, where wood/charcoal fires provided for heating and cooking. The black granite-framed fireplace (*danro*) is self-circulating to meet smoke emission standards. On the hearth are a Japanese black lacquer (*urushi*) teapot (*kyusu*) and a tray to the right, and candlesticks (*shokudai*) to the left. On the mantle are a reddish black lacquer bowl (*hachi*) on a stand to the left and a black lacquer (*urushi*) three-tray lunch or *bento hako* to the right. Windows on either side of fireplace (*danro*) are covered with reed *shojis,* while the window to the left has a reed blind or *sudare* as its window treatment. Also, on either side there are circular lamps called *andons*, which, when lit by *geishas*, let others know a room was occupied. *Obis* hang from the side walls of the alcoves on either side of the fireplace. The wood block print above the fireplace is a 1991 print entitled "Butterflies and Girl" by Tadashi Nakayama, a contemporary Japanese artist. Above the leather couch, the six-panel folding screen (*byobu*) from the early Meji period (1868 – 1912) has traditional Japanese subjects: cranes, stream, pine trees, and stream. At each end of the couch are Korean elm (*nire*) wood *tansus* with *obi* runners. A celadon lamp is atop the *tansu* to the right. Covers of the pillows on the couch are from *obis.* The coffee table in the middle of the room is a Japanese storehouse door or *kura*. Storehouses were typically attached to a Japanese house and stored family valuables including rice (*kome*). On the *kura* are *imari* bowls or *hachi* and a Chinese box made from Chinese vase chards. The two chairs in the foreground are from Chiang Mei, Thailand, and are carved wooden elephant chairs with *obi*-covered cushions and pillows. Between the chairs are a stack of Japanese floor cushions or *zabuton*, which are reversible, i.e., blue/white on one side and brown/white on the other. The low wooden chest to the left of the chairs is a Kanto design, copper-lined *hibachi*. *Tansu* in the left corner has an *obi* runner with a Toko Shinoda wood block print above with blue/white *imari hibachi* at its side. On top are a Thai bronze ware beggar bowl, a large cut glass vase, and a Japanese fan (*sensu*). Large and small Oriental rugs complete the decor. *Photo by Rod Hanna*

The hallway (*hiro-en engawa)* runs the length of north side of house along east-west axis. From the *minka* are pine (*matsu*) floor boards (*age-ita*), posts (*joya-hashira*), and beams (*bari*).The large chest is the base of a *futon tansu*, which is used to store *futons* and other bedding. The top is used in the great room as a buffet and for storage. Two *fukuro obis* adorn the top of the *futon tansu* as runners, as well as two small bronze temple lanterns (*seido-toro*), a red lacquer (*urushi*) covered bowl with turtle motif, and a blue/white *Imari* plate. Painted in the late Edo Period (1603 – 1867), a six-panel folding screen (*byobu*) depicts a woodland scene, including cranes *(tsuru*), bamboo *(take)*, stream *(ogawa*), low hills (*koyama*), cherry blossoms (*sakura*), chrysanthemums (*kiku*), and pine trees (*matsu*). A hanging *fukuro obi* includes a phoenix motif. The *kimono* print at the left is by Karen Young. At far end of hallway are the entry (*genkan*) and dining room (*chanoma*). *Photo by Rod Hanna*

The white silk wedding *kimono* is the focal point of the stairway. The display shelf was created from space between 8-foot ceilings of the powder room and closet below 10-feet normal ceilings of the first floor. In the display shelf are a Thai Buddha, a lacquer teapot (*kyusu*), an *imari* bowl (*hachi*), a large lacquer-covered rice bowl, and a Japanese textile as a runner. The print on the wall is a triptych or *sammai-tsuzuki* or three prints side by side. It depicts a battle scene between Japanese and Chinese with the Japanese being victorious. *Photo by Rod Hanna*

The 10-foot high ceiling in the sitting area is part of the south side interior veranda/hallway or *hiro-en engawa*. In the foreground is a chrome and glass Knoll Barcelona coffee table with an *Imari* bowl (*hachi*) on top and an Oriental rug below. Pillows on the sofa are Thai silk Jim Thompson pillows from Bangkok. The red lacquer *shoji* doors to the left are from the *minka* and open to the master bedroom. A *kimono* stand (*iko*) with *obis* hanging is further along left side. Above the *oki* is a black lacquer framed *ranma* with small pine trees *(matsu*) in the carved area. At the rear is an *obi*-covered metal-lined tea box (*ocha hako*) in front of a reed *shoji* door, which serves as a room divider to the master bath. Above is a black lacquer framed *ranma* with three carved flying cranes (*tsuru*). On the right side is a Regina music box from the 1880s, which plays large metal discs. On its top is a large blue/white *imari* plate (*sara*) on a stand. Beyond the music box on the floor is a wooden frame hearth or *irori* from the *minka*. Above the raked sand in the *irori*, a steel kettle (*chawan*) hangs from a *jizai kagi* (hook) attached to ceiling by a pulley (*kassha*) from the *minka*. The large curved beam was one of two main beams from the *minka* and is called the *ushi-bari*. It is supported by the main post or *daikoku-bashira*. The cross beams are called *chona-bari*. The wooden floor boards or *age-ita* are from the *minka*. *Photo by Rod Hanna*

The focal points in the whirlpool bath or *furo* are *subare* (reed shades covering windows). The shower is at the extreme left while a gas fireplace is at the right between his/her closets (not shown). The transom windows continue the overall theme of house. There are dark chocolate colored, marble counter top vanities, and a chaise with Jim Thompson silk pillows. An *obi*-covered tea box and *ranma* complete the picture. All beams and posts in this room are natural cherry (*sakura*) as is all new trim in the house. *Photo by Rod Hanna*

The main *minka* beam runs down the left side of room. Notches in the beams formed support for grate above the *irori* in the floor to allow smoke to rise into the second floor of *minka* and vent out through roof. The contemporary Japanese print of irises above the gas fireplace is by Sugiyama. An ornate porcelain Japanese incense burner is on the mantle to the right, and a *obi*-covered pillow is in the chair. Beyond the left of couch are a blue/white hibachi and a celadon beggar bowl from Thailand, along with red lacquer ware plates and boxes. The room also contains a Pakistani Bokara rug, *obi*-covered headboard, Chinese scrolls on either side of bed, a black lacquer folding screen above bed, and a Japanese lamp resting on the bottom half of tansu with *obi* runner. *Photo by Rod Hanna*

Renovating in an Asian Style

Architects and designers are often asked to renovate residences to reflect new tastes. Interior details reflecting Asian influence often can be seen in the orientation of the house on a site, integration of interior with the exterior environment, use and organization of space, and craftsmanship. Asian design elements range from the Chinese highly stylized furnishings , lacquered finishes, brightly colored accessories and statues of animals or mythical creatures to the more spare Japanese *shoji* screens, *tatami* mats, futons, and low profile tables to the ornate craftsmanship of India.

* We discovered several of these items at Pan Zhai, Rhode Island. *Courtesy of D. Peter Lund*

Zen Remodel

The entry space is deliberately designed to welcome and transition the visitor from the outside world into a quiet and embracing world. An entry water garden, which includes a meditation pagoda, emphasizes the Asian theme on either side of the long exterior corridor. Water gently cascades down the rock wall leading through the water garden to the front door so that visitors are embraced with calm, good luck, and positive thoughts. *Photography: Western Exposure*

This quiet meditative pagoda is secreted in the interior private water garden, where the simplicity of its surroundings provides an immediate disconnection from earthly cares. The gentle flow of water that surrounds this space is further enhanced by plants, which add a life force to the *Zen* environment. The combination of stone, copper, wood, and water bring nature and strength of well being into the environment. *Photography: Will Hare Photography*

Brion Jeannette evoked a *Zen* environment in redesigning this home. The existing house had great bone structure and good solar orientation. Using sustainable building materials and green technologies, the new design provides for a seamless transition between the natural beauty and peacefulness of the bay and the interior of the home. Long roof overhangs soften and enhance natural day lighting, creating a peaceful positive *chi*. *Photography: Eric Figge Photography*

Previously a dark room, this office is now open to the courtyard. It incorporates antique Chinese furniture and built-ins. When not in use, all electronic equipment is hidden away to create a relaxing space that allows for contemplation. *Photography: Western Exposure*

The use of a stone sink, bamboo faucet, and stonewalls continues the constant thread of nature throughout the house. *Photography: Western Exposure*

This home blends the clean simplicity of Asian lines with western materials and modern green technology. Exterior glass walls push completely open and out of sight. The result is a seamless flow that embraces nature, natural light, and ventilation in a quiet peaceful atmosphere. *Photography: Western Exposure*

Whether you are reading a book, embracing the warmth of the sun, or just taking in the views, the obvious result is comfort of mind and body. *Photography: Western Exposure*

The positioning of the bed wall employs *feng shui* principles. The foot of the bed does not point toward the windows or door; allowing the power of *chi* to remain within the bedroom. Note the bedside chest. *Photography: Western Exposure*

The spatial comforts of this bathroom embrace a positive *chi*. *Photography: Western Exposure*

This residence with its solar-heated horizon edge pool and elevated Japanese soaking spa are a compliment to the spectacular bay and sunset views. Day or night, this is a delightful way to find to peace and perspective.
Photography: Western Exposure

Asian Townhouse in Rosslyn

An expectant couple bought a four-story colonial townhouse in Rosslyn, close to Key Bridge. Both had lived abroad and traveled extensively and were convinced that, though the size and location of the house were ideal, the interiors could not stay. Andreas Charalambous of FORMA Design brought inspired touches of their Taiwanese/Vietnamese background into the house. In the entry foyer, a Buddha statue is perched on a pedestal above a cabinet that houses slippers for all who enter. As is customary in Asian houses, outdoor shoes are not worn in the house. *Courtesy of Geoffrey Hodgon Photography*

A two-sided Venetian plaster fireplace wall also holds a recessed plasma screen. All television equipment, CDs, and DVDs are stored in the dark chocolate-stained floor-to-ceiling cabinet that separates the Venetian plaster mass from the red accent wall. *Courtesy of Geoffrey Hodgon Photography*

A Chinese red wall, red for good luck, ties all the public areas together: living room, dining room, and kitchen. Low, neutral furniture with built-in side tables sits above a wool and silk handmade Cha-Cha rug by FORMAonline.com. Artwork by the architect, AndreasCharalambous.com, provides a finishing touch. *Courtesy of Geoffrey Hodgon Photography*

Lacquered cabinets, quartz countertops, and glass appliances shine in this Asian modern kitchen. A glass backsplash protects the red wall beneath. The floor is ebonized. *Courtesy of Geoffrey Hodgon Photography*

FORMA improved the flow of the space, opening up the layout to the abundant light coming from both the front and the back of the house, and bringing the space to its potential. The red wall and dark floors, beautiful lighting, and low furniture create the *Zen* feeling the clients wished for. *Courtesy of Geoffrey Hodgon Photography*

Natural light from a large window wall animates this master bedroom. The custom king-size bed dominates the main wall, which is painted a deep earth tone. The chaise and wool and silk handmade Cha-Cha rug from FORMAonline.com anchor this visually rich retreat. *Courtesy of Geoffrey Hodgon Photography*

A custom-designed sycamore wall incorporates a fireplace and plasma TV in this dressing and living area within the master bedroom. Dimmable ceiling lights, sconces, and floor and table lamps allow for a variety of moods. The dark, ebonized floor anchors the light walls and furniture in this master bedroom. *Courtesy of Geoffrey Hodgon Photography*

This restful guest bedroom, mostly for the visiting Asian in-laws, features a cozy niche for the bed, creating a sheltered feeling. Red is used behind the bed, in the crimson chaise and ottoman, as well as the artwork. *Courtesy of Geoffrey Hodgon Photography*

An uninterrupted mirror on one wall of this master bathroom reflects the glass shower enclosure, which makes the space feel very open. Echoing the shape and style of the shower, the toilet compartment features a sandblasted door for privacy. A double vanity and dark-stained floating cabinet and Asian-inspired elongated porcelain tile floors throughout complete this modern bathroom. *Courtesy of Geoffrey Hodgon Photography*

Tranquility at Monarch Bay

ADI Design Group, Inc. renovated this home in Monarch Beach, California. The hardwood front entry door with beveled glass inserts is one of the few original items remaining. Stepping stones lead you to the front entry stone landing, where flanking bamboo plants grow to the open sky. The center courtyard is visible beyond. *Courtesy of Sandy Noborikawa, Homeowner*

The house has a "U" shape floor plan with a Japanese garden in the center. With floor-to-ceiling windows and doors, a hall around the exterior of the house brings the outside garden into the home. *Courtesy of Sandy Noborikawa, Homeowner*

The neutral color scheme used in the building materials enhances the tranquil feeling of the space. *Courtesy of Sandy Noborikawa, Homeowner*

The living room offers views into the garden and towards Monarch Beach. Sliding doors and windows lead you toward the outdoor lanai with its ipe wood decking. *Courtesy of Sandy Noborikawa, Homeowner*

The dining room has a clean and simple appearance. *Courtesy of Sandy Noborikawa, Homeowner*

Floor-to-ceiling doors and windows give you sunsets and ocean views. Nature surrounds you here. *Courtesy of Sandy Noborikawa, Homeowner*

Asian Modern

Remodel West reconfigured a standard 1970s Sunnyvale, California, ranch home in the heart of Silicon Valley. Their design created an open kitchen/family room plan with adjoining dining and living rooms. The dining and living rooms house new furniture, fireplace, windows, and doors designed and specified by Remodel West. Expanding the existing house, relocating the kitchen and family rooms, and adding a new dining room achieved the clients' primary goals. They also provided a covered outdoor living area, lighting, and a seamless transition to the backyard with steps and columns that complement the house and add to its character. *Courtesy of Mert Carpenter Photography*

The clients desired to allow traditional Asian design and materials influence the contemporary style, and the design team responded with a blend of simplistic lines and warm materials. The overall layout of the kitchen allows for multiple cooks to work in the kitchen at one time while also entertaining their guests. The large island with varied dining and bar levels houses different groups of people at one time and allows for multiple functions. *Courtesy of Mert Carpenter Photography*

The finishes used to create the open kitchen complement the Asian style of the house with simple lines and striking materials, such as glass tiles mixed with slate. The columns are dressed to continue the look into the family room with their detail that coordinates with the cabinetry. The nearby built-in area for TV and stereo equipment completes the look and also gives the clients what they were looking for: a unique, custom piece designed to meet their needs and to suit their style. *Courtesy of Mert Carpenter Photography*

Asian Duplex

The client wished to provide a modern setting for her furniture and art collection; to create a dynamic state-of-the-art kitchen; and to develop a master bedroom/master bath suite that evoked her multiple trips to and affinity for Asia. FORMA Design unified the entry foyer/living/dining and kitchen areas of her 70s duplex apartment through the use of continuous maple floors, uninterrupted ceiling planes, and consistent halogen lighting. *Courtesy of Geoffrey Hodgon Photography*

Continuity in materials and lighting quality, as well as elimination of the previously existing doorways and fractured moldings, makes the space flow uninterrupted. A chocolate brown stained slab of wood replaced the traditional mantel. *Courtesy of Geoffrey Hodgon Photography*

The opening to the kitchen was enlarged, all the way to the ceiling, and the floors of the living room continue into the kitchen, making it feel part of the "entertainment" area. The same halogen lighting, always on dimmers, allows for the "moody" atmosphere to continue throughout the house. *Courtesy of Geoffrey Hodgon Photography*

The modern furniture from B&B Italia (red for good luck), the wall-to-wall linen curtains, and the artwork from AndreasCharalambous.com complete the simple yet powerful layout of the living room. Views of the lit Washington Monument at night make this space sublime. *Courtesy of Geoffrey Hodgon Photography*

Horizontal Poliform cabinets in matt laminate and sandblasted glass, a sandblasted glass backsplash, and stainless steel appliances make this chef's kitchen a dream. *Courtesy of Geoffrey Hodgon Photography*

The master bath continues the Asian feel. A huge walk-in glass enclosed shower with multiple temperature controlled showerheads, custom wenge floating cabinetry, ceramic mosaic tile, and an oversized mirror framed in the same wenge wood bring the "spa" feeling into the bath. Bath accessories collected during the client's trips to Asia bring back treasured *Zen* memories. *Courtesy of Geoffrey Hodgon Photography*

A drywall extension with carved tea-light shelves becomes a dramatic backdrop in the master bedroom. Japanese *shoji* screens cover the closets, and Japanese paper shades cover the windows. *Courtesy of Geoffrey Hodgon Photography*

Asian Aesthetic

Darryl Tucker of Helicon Hall Design Associates designed and restructured the first level of this twenty-five year-old passive solar house. In order for the former family room to be used as a dining room, Helicon Hall designed a sideboard to work as a room divider and *shoji* type panels to partially screen the new dining room from the foyer. Constructed of cherry, bronze glass, and rice paper/glass, they also allow the light to filter through. The original terra cotta stone floor seamlessly transitions to the new wood floor of the new kitchen. A honed mosaic marble border unifies the two floors. *Photography by Wing Wong/Memories TTL, LLC*

The former kitchen was too small. The new dining room eliminates a wall between the existing kitchen and former dining room to create a new 15 x 32 foot kitchen/breakfast room. *Photography by Wing Wong/Memories TTL, LLC*

The *shoji* panels used on the dining room sideboard were also used as a floor-to-ceiling divider to partially screen the kitchen from the new dining room. The *shoji* panel design is continued on the upper glass doors of the breakfast room cabinets. *Photography by Wing Wong/Memories TTL, LLC*

The clients wanted the space to have a better flow. The new entertainment room is a combination home theater and conversation area around the fireplace–two steps down from the new kitchen/breakfast room. The audiovisual cabinetry was designed with Asian elements. Antique Asian furnishings and accessories add to the overall ambience. A geometric ceiling cove completes the room, with a multi-layered lighting plan used throughout the renovated first level. *Photography by Wing Wong/Memories TTL, LLC*

East and West Blend

Brion Jeannette's design goal was to blend the neighborhood's exterior fabric with the owner's preference for simple Asian lines. Once inside the entry gate, it becomes immediately clear that you have entered another world, where the landscape provides a sense of intimacy. Brion Jeanette refashioned the original 1960s ranch style home into a *Zen* atmosphere, incorporating a variety of green techniques, which suit the Asian concept that less is more. *Photo by Eric Figge Photography*

The water garden entry with crooked, "zigzag" stepping pads infuse a sense of delight and peacefulness; welcoming good *chi*. Like removing your shoes before entering, this entry allows visitors to remove the cares of daily life as they prepare to enter the home. The water feature is home to a variety of very happy koi. Koi represents wealth and prosperity (from the Chinese pronunciation which is similar to 'abundance'). Together, the water and koi are used to energize the joy of living and symbolizes good luck in abundance as a welcome greeting to family and guests. *Photo by Eric Figge Photography*

The openness felt when traversing across the "zig-zag" entry water garden is enhanced by the welcoming open living room that beckons you to settle in simple comfort or pulls you out to the quiet and minimal landscape facing the Pacific Ocean; here, the Pacific Ocean is nourishment for the soul. In maintaining the simplicity of Asian form, Brion Jeannette has carried the beautiful wood ceiling and stone floor materials all the way through the inside and outside of the house. *Photo by Eric Figge Photography*

This bright and beautifully simple master bedroom enjoys natural light and ventilation through large ocean-facing windows and doors that allow the peaceful outside garden to become one with the beginning and ending of the owner's day. *Photo by Eric Figge Photography*

This open kitchen is infused with plenty of natural light and ventilation from operable north facing skylights that provide a gentle illumination. Accent finish colors with soft lighting have been employed to relate to the richness of Asian materials. To accent the clean, simple and uncluttered lines, wood paneling has been crafted to conceal appliances and create a sense of harmony. *Photo by Eric Figge Photography*

The master bath is washed with natural light, from the bow windows that bring the spectacular quiet ocean views into conscious focus to the large skylights that bring sunshine directly into this refreshing space. The openness of the shower and tub allow a sense of undisturbed continuance. A cascading water wall feature, simple wood slats, and a discrete fireplace add a feeling of serenity. *Photo by Eric Figge Photography*

This minimal landscape design utilizes California native plant materials and maximizes the beauty of the Pacific Ocean. The deep patio overhang is an extension of the interior living room ceiling and provides protection from the southwestern sun exposure while also blending the home's interior to the exterior. An infinity pool blurs the distinction between patio edge and the ocean beyond, adding a sense of calm. *Photo by Eric Figge Photography*

Tahitian Style

From the top of the stairs, you can see the swimming pool that travels under the exterior wall into the living room space. A small waterfall from the living room rocks fills the swimming pool. *Courtesy of Jim Buckley*

The front deck of this ADI Design Group, Inc., renovated home offers a beautiful view of Honolulu's south coast. The deck is covered with quartzite, and the wood bench is made from ipe wood. The fascia and door header are hand carved in Asia and reassembled in Hawaii. *Courtesy of Jim Buckley*

The hand-carved Asian column in the living room was designed and carved in Asia and then shipped to Hawaii. *Courtesy of Jim Buckley*

ADI used custom maple shaker doors for the kitchen cupboards. The hardware is *tansu* cabinet hardware from Japan. Hawaiian koa wood covers the floors. *Courtesy of Jim Buckley*

The homeowner delighted in the shape of the overall Tahitian style roof composed of a hand cut wood shake from the Philippines. It is also commonly known as a canoe roof because you can fit a hanging canoe in the interior ceiling space. The patio is a favorite relaxing space. *Courtesy of Jim Buckley*

Asian Inspiration

The client told Feinmann Inc. that they wanted a multi-purpose addition to meet several needs: a functional yet spacious home office similar to a Japanese "scholar's study," a beautiful entry way into the home, and a serene sitting area. The architecture of the existing home was in the Eichler style, also referred to as "California Modern," which developed in the 1950s. Such buildings feature low, sloped roofs, post and beam construction, and spaces that open onto nature. Clean modernist lines characterize the spaces, and the layout is based on an open floor plan common to both Wright- and Bauhaus-influenced architecture. This view of the entry along the plane of carport "screen" wall shows how the rhythm of lighting fixtures at the exterior continues inside along entry axis. The aesthetic of fixture reiterates both the interior and exterior *shoji* pattern. *Photography John Horner*

The *shoji*-like kalwall provides diffused, natural lighting into a living space through a translucent sandwich panel. It has the same insulating properties as a typical exterior wall and is considered to be a great "green" building material. This view of the *shoji*-like kalwall shows how the translucent wall acts as welcoming beacon/lantern as dusk falls. *Photography John Horner*

The entry hall is flanked by the kalwall to the exterior side and *shoji* screens to the other. *Photography John Horner*

Actual *shoji* screens enclose the scholar's study, which also doubles as a guest room. An antique Korean *tansu* can be seen on the right-hand side. Post and beam construction was continued from the existing house, preserving continuity with the original design aesthetic. *Photography John Horner*

View from study/guest room showing juxtaposition of the *shoji* and kalwall and their respective translucent qualities. *Photography John Horner*

Storage units were built into the space where the raised second floor of original building left a gap between that level and floor level of addition. The ceiling references traditional Japanese architecture. The outside lattice structure continues the horizontal pattern of the walls. The completed addition, which the homeowner has dubbed "the Japanese wing," provides the added space needed, while blending the inspirations of all the design sources: Asian and Western. *Photography John Horner*

Garden Pavilion

In designing an addition to a traditional home, DeLong and Stahl Planning and Design reflected the clients' fondness for reduced, minimalist Japanese design. In this pre-addition view, the long, narrow, and underutilized garden has no real connection to the home and the dark-hole-patio. The integration of the home and its environment was the underlying theme of this project. *Courtesy of DeLong and Stahl Planning and Design*

The patio was at the level of the house, elevated about 3 feet above the backyard. By placing the new bedroom, a perfect 18-foot by 18-foot square, in the center of the backyard on the diagonal, the firm created three exterior "garden rooms," defined spaces for defined purposes (see Chapter 5, "Eclectic Craftsman"). *Courtesy of DeLong and Stahl Planning and Design*

The wide overhang that extends into the interior as soffit (used to light up the ceiling), the mitered corner windows, and the ample use of wood paneling (Douglas fir) for the exterior and interior are design elements that James DeLong has used throughout his career. *Courtesy of DeLong and Stahl Planning and Design*

The light-filled gallery connects the master bedroom with the existing house. The niche above the return air grille (at the bedroom entry) displays Bali stick figures. At the far end, mitered-corner glass panels allow for an unobstructed view of the garden all the way from the existing house. *Courtesy of DeLong and Stahl Planning and Design*

The up lighted, rising ceiling, together with the openness of the space (windows in every wall except where the bed is placed), gives the master bedroom a light and airy feeling—very different from a "bedroom" but consistent with the actual use of the space—a garden living room, a space that is more part of the garden than the house. Similar to a Japanese tea pavilion, this space is open to the garden on three sides and three corners and just happens to have glass in those openings to protect the inhabitants! *Courtesy of DeLong and Stahl Planning and Design*

In the master bath, two hand-painted porcelain vessels rest on the modified 90-year-old Chinese altar table that serves as the vanity. Teakwood (a type of sandstone) floor and wall complements the colors of the Douglas fir trim and soffit. The addition's flooring and roof seamlessly continue from the existing building. *Courtesy of DeLong and Stahl Planning and Design*

The exterior garden rooms include the garden area off the patio, the pool area, with a trellised private patio, and the hidden garden, a tranquil, shaded area between the spa and addition. *Courtesy of DeLong and Stahl Planning and Design*

New Roots

Living on the Atlantic Ocean is beautiful: from the first tender green days of spring to those warm June days when boats fill the view to winter when snowflakes fall on the murmuring water. This forty-year-old house stretches lazily over the ocean. When the current owners bought it, they, their builder, and designer, Nancy Taylor, decided to take it back to its original frame and build it to suit their lifestyle. The renovated house had to accommodate Asian antiques, pieces of art, and an active family. The entry foyer has two matching Asian tables topped with unique bird sculptures. *Courtesy of D. Peter Lund*

The large living room affords dramatic views of the ocean. The blend of New England and Asian traditions and furniture is readily apparent. The fabric for the draperies is hand embroidered with ferns on a linen background and made in India. The treatments were fabricated in Rhode Island. Note the small Asian end table carefully placed at the end of the sofa and the Asian bowl on the table. *Courtesy of D. Peter Lund*

On the front of the house, the media room contains a Chinese day bed—perfect for watching old movies. *Courtesy of D. Peter Lund*

The richly paneled library is a wonderful place to play a game of cards on a rainy summer day. The game table is Chinese. *Courtesy of D. Peter Lund*

The white dining room overlooks the ocean. The delicately patterned fabric for the curtains came from Switzerland. *Courtesy of D. Peter Lund*

A bird sculpture and an elegant two-paneled screen top the antique Asian chest. *Courtesy of D. Peter Lund*

A lustrous painting of a lily pond hangs over the fireplace. Nearby is a four-paneled standing screen from Hong Kong. *Courtesy of D. Peter Lund*

The breakfast area with its chocolate brown walls boasts a Chinese chest and two modern paintings. *Courtesy of Nancy Taylor*

A Chinese chest and New England lantern are in juxtaposition. *Courtesy of D. Peter Lund*

An altar table punctuates one end. *Courtesy of D. Peter Lund*

A large meditation/relaxation/exercise room dominates the first level. Columns and Chinese decorative items accentuate the length of the lap pool. The room has several alcoves for sitting, playing cards, or enjoying the tranquility. *Courtesy of D. Peter Lund*

Elegant oils and Asian furniture break up the length of the second floor hall. *Courtesy of D. Peter Lund*

The boys' room is decorated in blue and white with bedding from China, featuring linen embroidered with penguins. *Courtesy of D. Peter Lund*

The girl's room is a pretty in pink. Notice the Chinese birdcage and the trunks. *Courtesy of D. Peter Lund*

The master bedroom contains a handsome Chinese desk under another lovely oil. *Courtesy of D. Peter Lund*

In designing this apartment, FORMA Design created a flow that permits you to enter the apartment on axis with a niche carved out of the sculptural red wall (an organizing element in the apartment) that, in turn, leads you into the living room. A cutout allows views into the kitchen and dining areas beyond. *Courtesy of Geoffrey Hodgon Photography*

In the living room, a low profile sectional sofa and ottoman over the Cha-Cha wool and silk area rug defines the primary sitting area, while a Cha-Cha concrete table from FORMAonline.com occupies part of the reading area by the window. *Courtesy of Geoffrey Hodgon Photography*

The wenge wood wall takes command of the living room with its vertical and horizontal light niches. It envelops the fireplace and incorporates the flat screen TV, as well as provides storage for all the audiovisual equipment. *Courtesy of Geoffrey Hodgon Photography*

The custom Cha-Cha headboard and floating nightstands takes command of the master bedroom suite with its hidden cover lighting. Giant pendant lights play up the drama. A Mediterranean color field diptych by the architect puts the finishing touch on the wall above the bed. *Courtesy of Geoffrey Hodgon Photography*

FORMA Design opened the enclosed kitchen and enclosed balcony cove in one open plan. The kitchen millwork continues as a backdrop to the dining area, incorporating open display shelving and buffet storage area below, while a secret door leads to the master bedroom suite beyond. The "Big Bang" is a pendant sculpture above the dining table. In the foreground, the concrete Cha-Cha table on casters and the walnut CH07 Shell chair by Hans J. Wegner create a cozy reading area. *Courtesy of Geoffrey Hodgon Photography*

Honolulu Harbor Twilight

The kitchen uses an inexpensive maple Shaker-style cabinets and moss green, handmade counter titles. The dark bronze door and drawer pulls have a hand forged look. In the background can be seen *shoji* doors, bamboo window covering, and a Noguchi rice paper light fixture. *Courtesy of Jim Buckley*

In this renovation, ADI Design Group, Inc., added an office area within the front entry hallway. The cabinet at the end of the hallway is a niche for artwork and also a bench to sit when removing shoes on entering the home. The footwear cabinet is located adjacent to the desk. *Courtesy of Jim Buckley*

The built-in bookcase sits side by side with the *shoji* doors. The *tansu* cabinet adds weight to the exquisite Japanese screen above. *Courtesy of Jim Buckley*

The Honolulu Harbor is basking in the twilight. The muted color scheme of the room allows the artwork to stand out and accent the space. The fabrics are of the same hue but with a subtle Asian pattern. The maple wood above the doors hides the concrete structural headers. *Courtesy of Jim Buckley*

Small Big House

This renovation and addition above an existing structure expand the experience of the house without physically making it bigger. SsD drew design influences from the Korean concept of *maru*, which translates into "semi-exterior, in-between space." Through the use of maru, the perception of the interior is broadened through views to either the greater landscape or to an intimate bamboo courtyard. By separating the rooftop addition into three pavilions, the voids between these volumes become just as important as the volumes themselves: It is this equilibrium between inside and outside that allows the experience of natural light, air, and views to become integral to the daily rituals of the house. The result is a residence where passive energy efficiency is intrinsic to the design. *Courtesy of SsD*

The high clerestory awning windows vent hot air, eliminating the need for mechanical cooling. Similarly through the use of overhangs, heat gain is reduced in the summer but harnessed in the winter. The radiant heated floors also borrow from the Korean tradition of *Ondol*, where heated floors save energy and relate the space to the earth. *Courtesy of SsD*

The newly introduced double height void brings natural light and air to the renovated living room, which once needed artificial lighting during the day. Moldings and decorative elements are stripped to maximize the reflective nature of daylight on planar surfaces. *Courtesy of SsD*

A bamboo garden separates and joins the guest bath and bedroom and becomes part of the interior landscape. *Courtesy of SsD*

Like traditional Korean architecture, the passageways are not just corridors but in-between spaces that invite encounters with nature. *Courtesy of SsD*

East Meets West

Charlene Bank Keogh

It is impossible to overstate the influence of the Asian aesthetic on our Western culture. As a designer, the Asian influences on noted architects and furniture designers such as Frank Lloyd Wright, Charles Rennie Mackintosh, and Greene and Greene were lessons I learned and absorbed. Wright's decision to open up the space within the interiors, blending rooms together, and yet, through the placement of furniture define a space within a space is legendary. Greene and Greene's sensitive, curved furniture and their use of the horizontal line evokes the Asian sensibility. The simplicity of Shaker furniture and the "form following function" characteristic of Stickley furniture are found in similar Asian furniture. These ideas were imprinted early on and were, at that time, the Western interpretation of Asian design.

With the increasing globalization of our world, trips, and even tenure in the East, Westerners are being directly exposed to Asian interiors, furniture, and culture. This globalization allows collectors to incorporate their Eastern exposure into their western lives through furniture, art, and objects. The marriage of these two worlds is amazingly natural. Now, there is no need to "interpret" the Asian aesthetic. We have found that the two styles can easily be married in a single room!

Westerners have also been exposed to the spiritual side of the Eastern world, most obviously through yoga, meditation, and religious studies. Once again, we have found that our home can be our refuge. Certainly, an inner sanctum is now needed more than ever with our ever-increasing chaotic, multi-tasking lives. The therapeutic influence of beauty and creativity in our home can have a profound effect on our well being. That psychology of simplifying our lives, seeing beauty in simple forms, and eschewing the clutter in our environments does influence the "clutter" in our minds—to experience objects representing extreme simplification is very refreshing. That is the wonderful Asian influence that we can incorporate into our daily lives.

The Asian idea of artistic value in everyday objects, hand craftsmanship, quality construction, straightforward materials, and ornament derived from nature is seen in our Arts and Crafts movement. Those values are now, in the twenty-first century, being appreciated more and more because artisans and craftsmen are a rapidly disappearing group of people. The beauty of hand-worked interiors and furniture, such as those made by George Nakashima and now his daughter, Mira, has an amazing ability for us to connect with ourselves, as we appreciate the care and craftsmanship that goes into creating a piece of furniture.

When we see the traditional Japanese style, we see a beauty that transcends cultural boundaries. This style underlies modern form and design in that it is profoundly influenced by simplicity, clarity, and lack of ornamentation. The repetition of pattern, reductive forms, the differing glances from inside to outside is uniquely Asian inspired. Japanese *shoji* screens change, with just the simple movement of the panels, what we see outside or how our space is configured. In Western culture, sliding panels of fabric or walls incorporate that same idea. The Japanese believe in having more than one use for a room. To edit out unnecessary items, keeping the space simple and reserved reflects the Asian spirituality.

In viewing the dining room, not only is it Asian inspired, but you can see how the Asian aesthetic has been incorporated into an interior in New York City. The *shoji* screens can be moved to change one's view of the expanse of New York City's lights, the urban equivalent to a garden. *Shoji* screens in Japan typically open to a real garden, bringing the outside in. The idea of a room within a room has been achieved through the use of an area rug and Mackintosh's high back chairs. When sitting at the table, the high backs of the chairs achieve the feeling of low walls around the table, creating an intimate environment within the large room. The three-panel room screen is mounted onto a wall as a piece of art. The art

Photo by Dan Muro, Fast Forward Unlimited

mounted on the back wall has the repetition of form found in Asian design.

With our extensive exposure to the Asian culture and its design aesthetics, we are able, without rejecting our Western ideas of comfort and design, to incorporate both East and West into our homes. Perhaps this very incorporation becomes a metaphor for our cultures blending together, the globalization of our world.

Ms. Keogh is the principal of her own firm, Keogh Design, Inc, established in 1988 in New York City. She has worked for major architectural and design firms prior to that time since 1974. Many of her New York City projects have received awards and been published.

Ms. Keogh earned her degree in Environmental Design from Pratt Institute. She worked under such notable designers as George Nelson and Ulrich Franzen. She currently resides in New York City with her husband, artist Charles Yoder.

4.
Designing in an Asian Style

Chinese cabinetmakers produced bamboo furniture, campaign chests, desks, trunks, and sea chests for the Western market from 1740 to 1870. Usually, they worked with Asian rose wood and what they called teak wood. They tended to design in Hepplewhite and Sheraton styles, adding obvious Asian touches such as dragon feet. The Western climate, however, was hard on the light woods, thin panels, and doors. Asian furniture is often insufficiently supported, which can result in warping and cracking. Today, classic Chinese furniture is enjoying a strong revival. Although Asian furniture tends to be functional, its chairs, chests, and cupboards can be works of art. Modern adaptations are based on centuries-old traditional designs.

Most Asian societies, as Michael Freeman points out in his beautiful work (2008, p. 46), highly appreciate the skill of a craftsman. They value the tactile impact of ceramics, stone, silk, lacquer, and wood. Great care goes into the design of the details from the delicate brushwork on a vase to the carving on a chest. Until the late twentieth century, Asian influence on Western decor was generally seen in an individual piece. Today, more Westerners are composing a distinctive Asian look using rich materials, handsomely crafted furniture, and contemporary lighting—rather than incorporating an Asian piece within their Western decor.

The growing knowledge of *feng shui* has resulted in a Western appreciation of the concept that design can create harmony in a space. To those who are accustomed to a more cluttered style, the practical beauty and less-is-more of this decorating style can be quite nourishing. Basically, *feng shui,* which literally translates to "wind and water," is an ancient Chinese art founded on the belief that our surroundings affect us. Its goal is to enhance the flow of *chi* (life force or spiritual energy), and to create harmonious environments that support health, beckon wealth, and invite happiness. *Feng shui* divides the world into five elements: wood, fire, earth, metal, and water. According to its principles, if you have a room that doesn't feel quite right, balancing the elements can make it more comfortable.

Many thanks to Tuulikki Loring, Trisha Traxler, and Pan Zhai for introducing us to these subjects.

The Flavor of the East

Charlene Keogh was asked to incorporate elements from the client's life in Asia and their furnishings from previous residences into a cohesive, modern, comfortable New York apartment high in the sky. She used Asian-inspired grass cloth on all the walls to unify the entire apartment and turned the wide foyer into an art gallery. A Japanese art hanging system allows the homeowner to readily change the art without disturbing the walls. The Japanese *tansu* chest in the foyer is from the late nineteenth/early twentieth century. *Dan Muro, Fast Forward Unlimited*

The *shoji* screens in the living room are positioned to allow a magnificent view of the city. Ming dynasty huanghauli (i.e., yellow flowering pear" wood) horseshoe armchairs are wed to a custom Frank Lloyd Wright-inspired coffee table by Charlene Keogh of Keogh Design. As the Asian esthetic inspired Wright, the apartment easily incorporated this style. The sofas are deliberately clean and simple in style. Charlene Keogh also designed the low back doublewide wingback chair. It is traditional in feel, with fun, ethnic fabric that neatly incorporates itself into the new environment. The zitan wood desk is from the late Ching period. *Dan Muro, Fast Forward Unlimited*

The dining area has dining chairs by Charles Rennie Mackintosh, who was also heavily influenced by the Asian esthetic. They blend beautifully with the Ming period altar table of huanghauli wood and the late Ching period chest centered on the window. Keogh Design created the dining room in the Mackintosh style as a response to the client's request to have an expandable table for large gatherings. The five photos over the altar table are by Lin Tian Miao. The designer, in conjunction with Stark Carpet, created the custom dyed rug for the dining area, using the greens and reds found in the antique rug in the living area. *Dan Muro, Fast Forward Unlimited*

Keogh designed the office/den like a ship's interior; every square inch has its purpose. The anigre woodwork incorporates varying heights of the windows, doors, and soffits to make all these elements appear blended together. The floating curved desk looks out to the Hudson River. *Dan Muro, Fast Forward Unlimited*

Sliding pocket doors incorporated into the entry allow the office to be closed off completely from the rest of the apartment. Keogh designed the custom sofa so it fit between the library bookcases, which contain the client's antique and Asian rock collections. The cabinetry also houses all the electronics for the entire apartment installed by Harvey Electronics. *Dan Muro, Fast Forward Unlimited*

The master bedroom incorporates *shoji* screens by Miyi, a traditional wing back chair covered in period Frank Lloyd Wright fabric, and traditional end tables, all blending with the late nineteenth century Japanese display chest. The custom colored carpet is by Stark and the bedding and pillows by The Susan Gil Workroom. *Dan Muro, Fast Forward Unlimited*

Asian Fusion in Brentwood

Estelle Jaivin ASID combines different Asian decorative arts in the interior design of this two-story town house in Brentwood, California. She framed the antique Chinese scroll depicting birds and rocks behind no-glare glass (for sun protection) and placed it on the wall to the right. An antique Indian bronze Buddha with halo is balanced by a sitting Indian bronze Buddha. On the stair wall are two, eighteenth century Japanese wall panels with mother of pearl, raised lacquer work, and chinoiserie. The"1000 Points of Light" chandelier emulates Chinese lanterns. *Courtesy of Estelle G. Jaivin ASID, CID*

The living room has a Chinese coffee table with burl wood top and lacquer base, which holds a reclining Buddha from India and a plant in an antique Thai monk's begging bowl on an old English stand. A pair of antique gilded Chinese foo dogs guards the room. On the far left wall is a pair of framed eighteenth century Japanese gift covers. The floor is hand-scraped hardwood oak. The lapis blue silk draperies lined with cinnabar red silk in theatre proscenium style reveal the garden and view. *Courtesy of Estelle G. Jaivin ASID, CID*

The living room wall displays framed seventeenth to nineteenth century antique Mandarin identity badges, along with a complete robe and skirt costume in the center. The boxed and French wired lamps on each side of the sofa are made from a pair of antique Chinese temple carvings gilded with 24-karat gold. Front left is a Chinese theatre doll; antique Chinese children's wedding gowns with decorative jade buttons are on the left wall. *Courtesy of Estelle G. Jaivin ASID, CID*

The guest bedroom contains an antique wood Indian temple carving (wall left, near table lamp) and antique glass-covered Indian *howdahs* (elephant seats), which serve as a pair of end tables. The framed antique Indian altar cloth behind the bed displays the four worlds of Buddha. The bedspread is made from new and antique trapunto embroideries. *Courtesy of Estelle G. Jaivin ASID, CID*

The powder room has a pair of custom crafted replicas of an antique Chinese lantern with jade finials. A Chinese silk painting (left) and a Chinese- style lacquer cinnabar cabinet accent the mirrored space. *Courtesy of Estelle G. Jaivin ASID, CID*

Teal Michel designed this residence. She used the Korean medicine chest in the entry as a storage area for keys, sunglasses, and other small items. The light beige loveseat is embroidered in a stylized chrysanthemum pattern. The Japanese view these popular flowers as a symbol of long life. The French fauteuil chairs sit on a silvery gray rug with a central Asian symbol. At the entrance is a standing blue and white porcelain vase with a lid topped with a foo dog. On the rose-colored, marble-topped decorative side table sits an antique blue and white porcelain Imari incense burner with a Shi-Shi final, c. 1850. Plum branches decorate the black lacquer and mirrored chest to the right of the love seat. A nineteenth century blue and white porcelain box sits on the glass-topped coffee table. Six antique black and white Chinese pen and ink drawings hang on the wall. To the left is a three-part colored antique wood block. *Courtesy of Teal Michel*

The two mid-1800 Japanese lacquer chairs have marble seats and inserts. With stylized clay and ball feet for the front legs, they were made for export to the western market. The lacquer chest and folding screen are newer pieces. *Courtesy of Teal Michel*

The artist signed the Japanese Sumei scroll of a geisha c. 1820-1830. *Courtesy of Teal Michel*

The family room has a monochromatic color scheme of intense reds: from the wall paint to the leather sofas, to the Bokhara rug with the typical "elephant foot print" symbol. Teal Michel commissioned the fireplace screen to be made with gold leaf and hand painted with a typical Asian-style landscape. The Chippendale style coffee table was inspired by Asian design. *Courtesy of Teal Michel*

Oriental paintings are turned into scrolls by surrounding them with subtle silken fabrics and backing them. They then can be hung on the wall or rolled up and displayed on special occasions. The Chinese Sumei scroll, c. 1870, has a landscape and water scene. *Courtesy of Teal Michel*

On the wall hangs a wall screen hanging, *thanka*, hand painted with vegetable dyes. This centuries old religious art form functions as a religious icon and a source of spiritual energy. The Asian red lacquer console holds a decorated Asian lidded woven basket typically used to hold rice. The accent chairs are made of bamboo, a strong building material used in Asian furnishings. *Courtesy of Teal Michel*

Teal Michel designed the headboard for this bed so that it framed five c. 1890 Chinese carved temple screens. Their carvings of birds and foliage inspired her design. To emphasize the bed, she mounted cobalt blue tile on the wall to frame it. The remaining furnishings carry the color palette of the room, including the wall scroll of an ancestor, an empress. To the left of the bed is a c.1885 Beijing red lacquer chest decorated with silkworms. To the right of the bed is a walnut chest c. 1795 from Hebei province. *Courtesy of Teal Michel*

Teal Michel designed this day bed, which incorporates two late 1800s Chinese temple carvings in the head and footboards. The bed is painted black to resemble the lacquer used in Asian furnishings. The wall scrolls include the lotus, a widely used symbol, and waterfowl. *Courtesy of Teal Michel* (above and opposite page)

Two Japanese *obis*, c. 1868-1902, hang from decorative cornices. The one on the left side is decorated with cranes and chrysanthemums, which symbolize long life. The center étagère holds a red lacquer lidded box with decorative gold painting, four small celadon vases on stands, a brown wicker tea box c. 1790, and small folded black lacquer screens decorated with Asian women. The red lacquer chest has a pottery Asian horse on top. The window treatment compliments the Oriental feel of the room. *Courtesy of Teal Michel*

Bombay Bachelor

A renovated fireplace using large rectangular tiles creates a contemporary *Zen*-like feel. *Fred Donham, Photographerlink*

This bachelor's home went from predictable traditional to authentic Asian with the help of Kerrie Kelly of All American Design & Furnishings, Inc. *Fred Donham, Photographerlink*

Simple repetition of artwork in the dining area provides just enough juxtaposition to the antique dining chair. *Fred Donham, Photographerlink*

In the breakfast nook, the clean-line banquette style seating with a lazy Susan round table is reminiscent of a traditional Asian family dining setting. *Fred Donham, Photographerlink*

House with a River View

FORMA Design transformed the subdued entry doorway of this riverside house with a splash of celadon. *Courtesy of Geoffrey Hodgon Photography*

The white concrete fireplace mass with the flat screen TV attached commands the center of the visual axis, while the indigo blue wall creates a dramatic backdrop. The custom Cha-Cha rug is from FORMAonline.com. The simplicity of the furniture selection against this backdrop helps create a comfortable *Zen* feeling. *Courtesy of Geoffrey Hodgon Photography*

The white artichoke pendant light creates a dramatic centerpiece floating above the glass and steel dining room table off the open kitchen and breakfast bar. *Courtesy of Geoffrey Hodgon Photography*

The open plan encompasses the kitchen, living, and dining areas, all sharing the sunlight pouring in from all directions, while allowing for the river views to be shared from every angle. *Courtesy of Geoffrey Hodgon Photography*

A minimally dropped ceiling defines the kitchen work area, with its breakfast bars. Light bamboo floors reflect the sunshine. *Courtesy of Geoffrey Hodgon Photography*

The counter play of the celadon wall in the background and the sun-dried tomato wall that separates the family room from the study set the scene in this comfy lower floor family room with French doors opening to the views of the Potomac river flowing below. *Courtesy of Geoffrey Hodgon Photography*

The stone fireplace surround with the hanging flat screen monitor becomes the focal point of the family room with the comfortable loungers that allow for long movie viewing in comfort. The study/guest bedroom lies beyond the sun-dried tomato wall with the pocket doors. *Courtesy of Geoffrey Hodgon Photography*

The custom floating millwork and concrete countertops help support the floating "his" and "hers" mirrors in this master bath facing the river. The sandblasted glass sheets have some areas mirrored and some clear. This technique permits the sunlight to stream in during the day, while always allowing for a mirrored surface for shaving or brushing. *Courtesy of Geoffrey Hodgon Photography*

The pebbled floor plays up the views of the river below. Glass partitions separate the shower and toilet compartments from the main bathing area, while sharing the sunlight streaming in. Playful cutouts in the privacy film separate the private from the semi-private areas. *Courtesy of Geoffrey Hodgon Photography*

The custom sun-dried tomato Cha-Cha rug from FORMAonline.com helps define the sitting area of this master bedroom suite, with uninterrupted views of the Potomac. Chaises flank a wenge wood long cocktail table on axis with the custom TV wall with the floating audio/visual cabinet. *Courtesy of Geoffrey Hodgon Photography*

China Rose

This room, as designed by Constance Holdip, LLC, is a colorful palette of jewel tones, abstract art, Asian floral designs, and vintage furnishings. The chaise has an array of pillows in gold, peach, emerald green, and chocolate. The sideboard near the window is filled with a contemporary floral design with various accessories. *Courtesy of Brenna King Photography*

A contemporary floral design in a ceramic orange and green vase creates drama and interest. *Courtesy of Brenna King Photography*

The floral design at the end of the chaise is a display of tulips and cymbidium orchids in a gourd sitting on a green taffeta-draped stand. *Courtesy of Brenna King Photography*

Stylish and fun, this room has a soft tan leather sofa with green accent pillows. The art is a 1950 black and white photo taken by a French photographer Robert Doisneau and enlarged. The faux crocodile trunk and leopard faux area rug add an eclectic mix to the room. *Courtesy of Brenna King Photography*

The bed has a deep red duvet, with a deep chocolate thrower, and gold accent pillows. On the wall is rich red silk with gold Chinese etchings wrapped around canvas. The brown leather parson side chair has accent pillows with a patchwork pillow to add contrast. *Courtesy of Brenna King Photography*

Oriental Retreat in Pasadena

Estelle Jaivin brought many Asian elements together in her design for the living room. On either side of the brass and glass cabinet, she positioned antique Japanese armorials. The cabinet contains a collection of antique Chinese and Japanese porcelains. The right hand wall features an eighteenth century Japanese four-panel hand painted silkscreen. On each side of the sofa, she placed antique Chinese wedding baskets to be used as end tables. On top of the Lucite Japanese-style coffee table is an Indian reclining Buddha. An antique *howdah* acts as a chair, and the floor lamp is made from an antique Chinese brass candlestick. A pair of Indian acolytes sits on each side of the fireplace. *Courtesy of Estelle G. Jaivin ASID, CID*

In designing this family room, Estelle Jaivin placed a hand painted, four-panel antique Japanese silkscreen on the left. Framed antique Chinese and Japanese textiles surround it. The wall is papered in Chinese grass cloth. The porcelain figure of a child on the floor is a nineteenth century antique Chinese sleeping pillow. *Courtesy of Estelle G. Jaivin ASID, CID*

In the master bedroom, Estelle Jaivin placed an eighteenth century rosewood opium bed with typical Chinese open fretwork. On the bed are an antique Chinese wedding gown and Chinese embroidered silk pillows. The nightstands are Chinese carved rosewood with a cloud and bird pattern. The side lamps are antique Chinese ormolu pots inlaid with semi precious stones. The rug with its contemporary leaf pattern was made in Thailand. Outside can be seen a Chinese stone lantern and Chinese-inspired lacquered wicker furniture. *Courtesy of Estelle G. Jaivin ASID, CID*

For the meditation room that was added to the residence later, Estelle Jaivin used Japanese *shoji* screens for walls and a wool area rug depicting a Chinese ocean wave pattern as the floor covering. Contemporary artwork with Japanese influences is on the left, and a Chinese scroll showing a water dragon is on the right. There is a bronze water sculpture, called "La Figura," on the right; "Innies and Outies" bronze sculptures used as end tables; and a faux rock masking a sound system speaker on the right. *Courtesy of Estelle G. Jaivin ASID, CID*

Chinese/New England Fusion

Many designers use Asian pieces as a counterpoint to exquisite furniture and other collectibles. In this large room, designer Tricia Traxler artfully combined various Asian pieces with family heirlooms. *Courtesy of D. Peter Lund*

In the eighteenth century, China produced the most intricate and stunning wallpapers in Europe and the American colonies. Researchers have found that Chinese homes did not have wallpaper; rather, Chinese merchants created sets of painted wallpaper to use as gifts to finalize deals with their European trading partners. These papers can still be seen in famous country houses, where they serve as backdrops for beautiful old furniture. In this case, the dining room in this old sea captain's house was little and looked out to the busy street. Designer Tricia Traxler thought this small but high-ceilinged dining room needed something smashing to overcome its street view. *Courtesy of D. Peter Lund*

She found a lovely bright Chinese wallpaper filled with exotically plumed birds. *Courtesy of D. Peter Lund*

Then she filled the room with exquisite New England antiques. *Courtesy of D. Peter Lund*

An important Asian product was lacquer. Japanese and Chinese chests often had large lacquer doors. Japanese lacquer had a flat, usually black glossy surface decorated in raised gold. Chinese lacquer was incised and often displayed ornate compositions such as seen here. Tricia Traxler placed this black lacquered headboard with scenes of teahouses and strolling lovers in a small narrow guest bedroom. To accentuate it further, she placed a brilliantly colored robe to hang over it. *Courtesy of D. Peter Lund*

Asian High Rise Paradise

Estelle Jaivin created a dramatic Chinese entry way in a high-rise condominium by using a Chinese Chippendale bench decorated with Chinese embroidered pillows, Chinese gilt bronze lamps showing a mystical Phoenix (symbol of life), and a four-panel coromandel screen. *Courtesy of Estelle G. Jaivin ASID, CID*

Asian Audio Cabinet

The client, an avid collector of Asian art and artifacts, needed an audio cabinet that would complement the other Asian influences in the room. In working on this piece, Reginald Thomas reflected nineteenth century and early Sung Dynasty furniture styling. Common characteristics for this style of furniture are simple forms made of hardwoods, beautifully finished, usually dark to reddish brown, usually non-ornamental, except for careful moldings and significant hardware. In this case, Thomas exaggerated some of the careful moldings at the cornice and base as well as the undulating counter element. He also added simple columns, providing a cultural link between the western and eastern vocabularies in the room and blending in smoothly with the eclectic surroundings.
Reginald L. Thomas Architect, LLC

Ethnic Eclectic

Kerrie Kelly of All American Design & Furnishings, Inc. helped her client design a more harmonious feel in her residence by contrasting light wood flooring with warm walls and woven furnishings. The combination of sleek with warm and woodsy elements provides a serene vibe with Asian flair. *Fred Donham, Photographerlink*

Bamboo dining table legs, specialty lighting, metals, and rich fabrics complete the look beautifully. *Fred Donham, Photographerlink*

The kitchen end of the Asian-inspired space uses very simple, clean lines. The decorative details are kept to a minimum, as in the very spare lines of the supporting column and cabinet doors. Colors span from the typical Japanese sage green of the walls to the deep Chinese red cabinets topped with matte black granite. The textural squares for the backsplash tiles are a common shape used in Japanese design. Even the pendant lights over the island would be right at home lighting a Japanese temple. *Photo by Audrey Vasey*

Donna Domenicali of Blue Heron Designs Inc. designed an Asian-inspired fireplace for an open-plan contemporary home near the Atlantic Ocean. The homeowners, who are avid hikers and mountain climbers, wanted a clean, spare look that reflected their love of nature. The previous asymmetrical fireplace and wall reeked of 1970s design, so Domenicali moved the wall planes to create a symmetrical facade and used contrasting textures – smooth Black Absolute honed granite from Zimbabwe and rough white Fond du Lac stone – to draw the eye. Inset into the granite surround are four square copper tiles that form a square. This motif, echoed in the cabinetry doorknobs flanking the fireplace, is often found in Japanese design and is reminiscent of the squares of a *shoji* screen. The perfectly aligned mantel and raised hearth, with their long horizontal line supported by short vertical lines, mimics the roof and supports of the Buddhist temple. *Photo by Audrey Vasey*

This *zen*-like nook invites the passerby to sit, relax and reflect by the sun-filled window. The simple lines of the woven leather bench mimic the roof and sides of a Buddhist temple, while the pillows could have been made from kimonos. Situated under a rough wooden staircase, the space borrows its play of textures from Asian design. *Photo by Audrey Vasey*

The black and spring green of this powder room are a common color combination found in Asian design. A *shoji* screen door is used on the vanity, and this Asian feel is echoed in the Japanese-style joinery on the mirror. Natural materials, such as the rough granite counter, the bronze of the Asian-influenced faucet spout, and the stone of the vessel sink further enhance the *zen* feel of this space. *Photo by Audrey Vasey*

As a frequent traveler to Asia, the client had a large collection of art and artifacts that needed to be shown to their best advantage. Blue Heron Designs Inc. created a backlit built-in display for the master bedroom that provides a great way to view the client's beloved pieces. *Photo by Audrey Vasey*

West Village Condominium

The client purchased a small condo overlooking the water in New York's fashionable West Village. Along with the new address came space restrictions and the building's contemporary architecture. Nicole Hogarty Designs created a modern, edited space, prioritizing scale and function. She selected a warm neutral palette for walls and fabrics and introduced textures and color in the wall coverings, the rich walnut tones of the furniture pieces, a sisal rug, and the bold contemporary pieces of art commissioned for the space. The custom walnut island attachment functions as dining table, buffet or desk. *Courtesy of Nicole Hagarty Designs* (above and opposite)

To compensate for a small master bedroom that did not allow enough space for a headboard, Nicole used two Asian screens above the bed. She placed an antique bamboo chair in the corner of bedroom in order to retain a full view of the city from all angles of the room. *Courtesy of Nicole Hagarty Designs*

The Oriental Touch

Miriam Ansell designed a formal living room in timeless shades of white, cream, silver, and gold. The classic room offers a quiet refuge during a busy day or a dramatic stage for entertaining where the guests are the center of attention. Chinese watercolors painted by the homeowner's mother (a biologist born in China) and the homeowner's cousin (an official restoration artist in the Imperial Palace Museum in Beijing) add an authentic touch of the Orient to this sophisticated salon. *©Photograph by David Van Scott. All Rights Reserved.*

An ebony Steinway in a sea of soothing shades of cream offers a visual anchor in the serene living room, subtly accented with a Chinese silk tapestry brought back from a visit to Suzhou and a custom-designed hand-woven silk and wool Tibetan rug. The living room also serves as a music drawing room used by all members of the family, and the annual Christmas party sing-along makes full use of the versatile seating plan: the fun faux fur bench on the left is always the first seat to be claimed! *©Photograph by David Van Scott. All Rights Reserved.*

East meets West in this cross-cultural dining room, melding Asian elements from one side of the family with the European traditions of the other. Chinese watercolors painted by renowned Chinese painter and calligrapher Qigong (above the fireplace) and the homeowner's mother combine with a collection of Chinese vases, each with its own story, to add a very personal touch. *©Photograph by David Van Scott. All Rights Reserved.*

Fans have played a functional, decorative and even ceremonial role in Chinese culture for over 3,000 years. This collection of fans with their distinctive light sandalwood scent lends a whimsical note to a formal dining room.

Old Meets New

The client requested Kerrie Kelly of All American Design & Furnishings, Inc. to incorporate some flair to the clean lines of this contemporary home. By using inherited family furniture pieces and elements discovered from family travels, Kelly transformed the wet bar and sideboard area. They now exude the family's personality. The combination of organic and hard-line elements provides the perfect yin and yang for the space. *Fred Donham, Photographerlink*

An Asian Space

Interior designer and allied ASID member, Danielle Orlowski has an eclectic theme in the living room. She draws accents from all over the world, including a red lacquered cabinet (not shown), solid wood coffee table, and a cloisonné vase from China; an elephant chair and a pair of praying statue from Thailand; Indonesian wood carved panels and bird lamp base; a Balinese parasol; Indian brocade; oil lamps; ancient rice vessels; *chapatti* box and rolls; and a Birman offering box. *Courtesy of Wing Wong, Memories TTL*

The opulent space has brilliantly colored fabrics like silk, embroidered velvet, and brocade. *Courtesy of Wing Wong, Memories TTL*

To make her dining room peaceful, she combined silk and linen fabrics, solid wood, ceramic, and bronze with earthy accessories such as branches, bark, potpourri, and shells. She chose neutral colors and minimalist furniture with an Asian feel, creating a space inspired by a Japanese *Zen* garden. The bamboo seen through the bay window emphasizes this idea and connects the setting to the outdoor. *Courtesy of Wing Wong, Memories TTL*

Asian Flare

The client requested Nina's Nuances Interior Design to create a wonder environment with an "Asian" flare in this 2,200 square-foot contemporary town house. The new design is a mix of Asian and contemporary styling that uses the principles of *feng shui*. The redesigned multi-use living room is sometimes used as an office: the desk and computer are contained within the wall unit. These two views show the off-centered placement and arrangement of the furnishings. *Courtesy of Wing Wong, Memories TTL*

The Asian-inspired look is a result of the rugs, owls, mirror, wall hangings and earth colors, which warm the environment. *Courtesy of Wing Wong, Memories TTL*

The *shoji* screen in this staircase conceals a center hall window, which faces the street. It also filters the light beautifully. *Courtesy of Wing Wong, Memories TTL*

Japanese-inspired Bedroom

This Japanese-inspired room is part of a Soho residence in New York City. Designed by Magdalena Keck, its highlights are a classic Isamu Noguchi floor lamp and Darren Almond's Sakura Full Moon C-print. The wood Japanese bed with Takashimaya natural linen sheets is surrounded by geometric, high contrast area rugs. *Courtesy of Chuck Choi*

Sensual Bedroom

A transparent woven steel mesh drape separates the sleeping area from the dressing area. The dressing area consists of two, chocolate brown, hand-woven leather cubed stools, an elegant stick and slate sculpture, and two closets. Both the closets are covered with canvas curtains backed with a sheer green willow leaf fabric to create a soft silhouette on the exterior and a delightful lace effect on the interior. The recessed halogen ceiling lights and the low voltage spot lighting create an ambient artistic atmosphere throughout the entire room. *Courtesy of Daniel Furon*

In the room's center is a custom solid walnut bed and bed table with a champagne and deep sage silk shantung and silk check coverlet, which provides an elegant richness to the sleeping area. A pair of square silk pillows portraying eighteenth century festivities flank a small silk check bolster in the middle of the bed. The lightly textured deep taupe walls with matching satin trim evoke serenity. Twelve vertical wall panels adorned with sculpted silver angels line one of the longer walls; a dimensional bamboo wall installation lines the other. The wall-to-wall carpeting is an off-white nylon pile, which reflects light and creates a pleasing contrast to the dark furnishings. Originally created as a kitchen sink, the modern zinc champagne table is placed on a complementary stand to serve as an artful piece of furniture. A tall fishtail plant and matte black pot complete the corner. *Courtesy of Daniel Furon*

This simple, sexy, serene room created by Elizabeth Brownrigg focuses on the union of opposites: light and shadow, intimacy and space, masculine and feminine, spirituality and sensuality. Nearly all of the elements are custom designed and hand crafted specifically for the room. The sliding Buddha and *shoji* screens serve as both a window treatment and as wall panels. The light-dependent images appear and disappear, depending on the time of day and the position of the panels. A delicate white silk curtain backed with a dragonfly sheer adds to the effect. *Courtesy of Daniel Furon*

Eastern Tradition Oceanfront Retreat

In the atrium, she used porcelain tile in a Chinese design for the floor and a Chinese Ching dynasty eight-panel coromandel screen. The Chinese-style McGuire sofa (bamboo/rawhide) is covered in faux Chinese embroidered ultra-suede. The room contains a pair of antique Chinese lacquered chairs and a round table with inlaid pearl design. A Chinese porcelain garden table is on the left near the sofa.
Courtesy of Estelle G. Jaivin ASID, CID

Estelle Jaivin designed this entryway by using a Chinese Ching dynasty eight-panel coromandel screen, an antique hand-loomed Indian Mogul rug, and a hand-painted Chinese scroll done in brush strokes showing a "water and rock" scene. *Courtesy of Estelle G. Jaivin ASID, CID*

Garden Yoga Studio

The client hired Forma Design to redesign the garden level of this home in the woods and transform it into a family room and yoga studio. A plasma screen over the fireplace shows instructional videos during the class, as the surround sound pumps new age music. An egg-shaped cocktail table becomes the shrine for a small statue of Buddha. An exterior cedar deck extends into the woods for a meditative after-yoga walk. *Courtesy of Geoffrey Hodgon Photography*

Natural and earth friendly materials in a neutral palette play up the *Zen* feeling throughout. Sliding *shoji* screens with translucent Plexiglas panels imbedded with natural grasses provide privacy during meditation. The bamboo flooring is heated from below in the winter. *Courtesy of Geoffrey Hodgon Photography*

The spiral staircase down from the main level was re-faced in light bamboo treads that match the bamboo floor below. The railing was simplified into a stainless steel and cable assembly. The abstract simplicity of the stair, as seen as you descend into the space, underscores the *Zen* feeling of the space. *Courtesy of Geoffrey Hodgon Photography*

Soon after their marriage, this couple was sent overseas to Japan in the late 1960s and then to Thailand in the early 1970s. There they purchased household items for the home they hoped to buy when they returned to the United States. Today, they use these items to decorate their attractive condominium. *Courtesy of D. Peter Lund*

The hibachi used in tea making and the *jisai no kagi* are used for decor. The latter is the cylindrical bamboo piece with a rod in the center that has a fish head at the end. Its purpose is to keep cooking vessels hot/warm over an open fire. *Courtesy of D. Peter Lund*

Sitting on the floor is common in Japan but some cushioning helps the comfort levels. The *zebulon* table is a functional and attractive piece of furniture. It stores cushions for additional seating. *Courtesy of D. Peter Lund*

This *tansu* stores a variety of household items. *Courtesy of William B. Ford*

5.
Landscaping in an Asian Style

India still has several magical gardens built by the Moguls, who loved large ornamental gardens. Their poets sang of their beauties; the air was always perfumed; and their designs were elaborate patterns. Today, most people agree that Japanese landscaping has the most elegant combination of essential elements. Certainly, it is beautiful. Modern landscape designers use Western construction techniques to blend Eastern and Western design into lush green havens of peace

Many thanks to D, Peter Lund and Elizabeth Schumacher of Garden Accents (West Conshohocken, Pennsylvania) for these images

Japanese Garden Landscape

Upon acquiring an adjacent hillside parcel of land next to their estate, the client called on Rios Clementi Hale Studios to redesign their outdoor quarters to unite the hillside with the existing property. The architects enhanced the driveway entering the estate by creating a large front lawn to give the house scale. The new entry takes drivers through the event lawn, providing glimpses of multiple gardens throughout, and ends at a motor court located just off of the main house. *Photo: John Ellis*

The walkway along the brick porch of the existing Tudor house ventures through a continuous garden to the front door. *Photo: John Ellis*

By linking paths through the hillside to various walkways across the grounds, the landscape architects lead visitors from the steep hillside gardens to the Japanese garden/outdoor living room and onto the large event lawn. While the outdoor setting is well equipped for entertaining, the space remains intimate enough for private use. *Photo: John Ellis*

To fulfill the clients' desire for space to entertain both large and intimate groups, the architects created the outdoor dining/living room, which is positioned between the main house and guesthouse. Outdoor furniture creates a comfortable living room setting complete with a fireplace, while brick flooring provides the foundation for the different exterior spaces. *Photo: John Ellis*

A wood-beam tennis pavilion with a steeply pitched shingled roof with Tudor nuances features a custom teak dining table for four. *Photo: John Ellis*

The extensive lawn connects every element of the estate and becomes the ideal location for large-scale events. The existing Japanese koi pond—adjacent to the main house—features a flowing waterfall that gently splashes onto floating lily pads below. The architects have skillfully incorporated the estate's natural surroundings, including mature chorisa and tall podocarpus trees, within the design of this outdoor oasis. *Photo: John Ellis*

Urban Zen Retreat

Joan Grabel of Park Slope Design designed this urban *Zen* retreat for a Los Angeles writer who wanted a sanctuary for relaxing and a place to write and entertain. The client had in mind a large red wall linking the two sitting areas of this urban retreat. Grabel designed an 8 x 6-foot high metal wall, painted Arabian red, with a niche to showcase Asian art. It is a dynamic backdrop for the helix-shaped black basalt water feature. Aqua colored stones and two agave parryi are at the base of the fountain. The grey/blue color of the agave integrates smoothly with the geometric bluestone of the patio. *Courtesy of Joan Grabel/Park Slope Design*

Bamboo, a symbol of longevity, surrounds this intimate outdoor room. Its sparse planting design expresses modern simplicity. *Courtesy of Joan Grabel/Park Slope Design*

Dwarf agave embedded in grey green stones compliments the vibrant red wall and mysterious black bamboo. *Courtesy of Joan Grabel/Park Slope Design*

Framed by black bamboo and anchored by a dynamic and inviting water feature, this urban oasis provides a tranquil retreat for a writer and a haven for humming birds, as well as an inviting space for luxurious nighttime entertaining. *Courtesy of Joan Grabel/Park Slope Design*

Honduran fired pottery and a Moroccan lantern blend seamlessly with the patio's *Zen* aesthetic. *Courtesy of Joan Grabel/Park Slope Design*

Asian Serenity in a Philadelphia Garden

Elizabeth Schumacher of Garden Accents appreciates the importance of garden ornaments in garden design. She has searched throughout the world for quality Asian pieces for her own award-winning garden. This antique stone wizened philosopher reflects amidst rocks and ground cover. *Courtesy of Elizabeth Schumacher's Garden Accents*

Bronze Mindanao knife holders now hold small begonias. *Courtesy of Elizabeth Schumacher's Garden Accents*

A stone Buddha stands at attention. *Courtesy of Elizabeth Schumacher's Garden Accents*

A Japanese teahouse draws the eye further into the garden. *Courtesy of Elizabeth Schumacher's Garden Accents*

An aged stone pagoda punctuates arrival at the next level of a terraced garden. *Courtesy of Elizabeth Schumacher's Garden Accents*

Monarch Bay Garden

As part of the house renovation (see Chapter 3), ADI Group redesigned this garden. *Photos Sandy Noborikawa, Homeowner*

Eclectic Craftsman

Joan Grabel of Park Slope Design designed an Asian-inspired landscape for this home renovation done in a Frank Lloyd Wright style by architects, Delong and Stahl. Working with the architects "Garden Pavilion" theme, the homeowners' interest in modern Japanese aesthetics and appreciation of Asian art, Grabel designed an eclectic landscape in keeping with Asian design principles. While shopping for the stone fountain, the clients took notice of these wonderful Balinese statues. The statues, framing the pool/spa horsetail wall, are reminiscent of guardians at the temple gate. *Courtesy of Joan Grabel/Park Slope Design*

The orderly repetition of shrubs and dark stones, often found in Japanese design, flows through the central garden expressing a neat, monochromatic palette. *Courtesy of Joan Grabel/Park Slope Design*

The mass of red blooming azaleas echoes a Japanese landscape in the spring. *Courtesy of Joan Grabel/Park Slope Design*

The water feature and bamboo, classical elements in a Japanese garden, are enhanced by the modern pavilion in the far garden room. *Courtesy of Joan Grabel/Park Slope Design*

Outdoor lighting in the garden and the house accent the serenity of the "Garden Pavilion" Asian-inspired architecture of the home and landscape. The home architecture is by Delong and Stahl (see Chapter 3). *Courtesy of DeLong and Stahl Planning and Design*

San Marino Landscape

Rios Clementi Hale Studios designed the landscape for a San Marino residence. *Photo: John Ellis*

Bluestone pavers, overgrown with creeping thyme, chamomile, dichondra, and herniaria, define the dining area. The dining area is furnished with a bright yellow dining table by Roy McMakin, with oversized McMakin chairs in varying shades of yellow. *Photo: John Ellis*

Their plan included distinct areas for living, dining, grilling, relaxing, and swimming. *Photo: John Ellis*

The concrete tile floor design resembling a Tibetan carpet defines the outdoor living room. This area is furnished with wrought iron furniture with Sunbrella-upholstered cushions and a wooden Moroccan table. *Photo: John Ellis*

A "wall" composed of a lush podocarpus hedge and a red-painted trellis of bamboo and cedar posts further defines the living area. Glass tile mural covers a door to a storage area for children's pool toys. *Photo: John Ellis*

Landscape architect David Tamura created this private Japanese garden. It is only visible from the husband's office, the wife's craft room, and the powder room. *Courtesy of Jim Buckley*

Private Japanese Garden

The koi fishpond has night blooming lilies and borders a quartz-ite stone driveway. The river rocks imitate a dry rock bed that lead to the hidden front entry door. *Courtesy of Jim Buckley*

6. Resources

ADI Design Group is an architectural and interior design firm specializing in high-end residential design. Formed in 1988, it has ten staff members who are capable of delivering a finished project – from drawings to specifications for door hardware. Project types include hospitality, federal military, office, medical, and high-end residential. The firm has worked on all the Hawaiian Islands, Japan, Korea, and California.
• 851 Pohukaina St., Building C, Bay 3, Honolulu, Hawaii 96813
• 808.593.8950 • paul@adihawaii.com
• www.adihawaii.com

For over a decade, **Blue Heron Designs Inc.** has been creating living environments that integrate clients' passions, accommodate their evolving lifestyle, and anticipate their future needs. This firm's knowledge and use of universal design and aging-in-place is evident throughout their projects, which have included designs for more leisure, entertaining and exercise activities, renovations to accommodate aging parents, building a weekend getaway, preparing for changing physical abilities, and downsizing. The firm's work has been featured in many publications.
• 510 West St., Long Branch, New Jersey 07740
• 732.263.1300 • info@blueheron-designs.com
• www.blueheron-designs.com

Brion Jeannette Architecture began in 1974 with a design philosophy focused on green architecture. The firm has spent 30+ years incorporating healthy building products, implementing passive and active solar strategies, and employing these techniques, generally without visible notice. Its projects range in scope from 2,500 square foot beach cottages to palaces around the world.
• 470 Old Newport Blvd. Newport Beach, California 92663
• 949.645.5854 • email@customarchitecture.com • www.customarchitecture.com

Elizabeth Brownrigg creates unique spaces in homes and businesses, combining her fine arts background with interior design and stagecraft. Her work ranges from commissioned pieces to site-specific installations. She is dedicated to helping people successfully transform a space into a creative, functional environment that's interesting and unique through beautiful art, interior design, or both. She has been featured on HGTV several times.
• 575.758.2758 • egb@elizabethbrownrigg.com
• www.elizabethbrownrigg.com

Carter+Burton Architecture P.L.C. is a small Virginia architecture firm that specializes in a few good projects per year. Located in Berryville, a small town one hour west of Washington, DC, its architects love to design and work within a wide range of budgets. The firm's focus is on quality, craftsmanship, and innovation. It tries to promote passive solar techniques and eco-friendly building materials.
• 11 W. Main St., Berryville, Virginia 22611
• 540.955.1644 • jim@carterburton.com
• www.carterburton.com

Clyde Reynolds Carpenter, FAIA, Architect, has received several design awards for his architectural projects and for the adaptive reuse of a nineteenth century carriage house as a modern living space. The latter has been published in several books and featured on national television programs. His work, ranging in scale from residential to ecclesiastical, maintains a sympathetic dialogue between contemporary modernist and traditional vernacular architecture. He is Chair of the Department of Historic Preservation and Professor in the School of Architecture at the University of Kentucky College of Design.
340 New St., Gratz Park, Lexington, Kentucky 40507
• 859.254.2140

James E. DeLong of **DeLong and Stahl, Inc.** has been building and remodeling residences since 1947, when he returned to Los Angeles after his apprenticeship with Frank Lloyd Wright in Taliesin, Wisconsin. Many of his houses are published; some are still inhabited by the original clients who still turn to Jim if the need for any change occurs. Since 2003, Jim DeLong has practiced in partnership with Thomas Stahl, who contributes his European sensibility, client focus, and twenty years of experience designing large scale projects. Together, they have planned numerous residential remodels and additions in the Los Angeles area.
• 1146 Morada Place, Altadena, California 91001
• 626.381.8944 • delong_stahl@earthlink.net

Estelle Jaivin & Associates is a full service interior architecture and design firm specializing in residential and executive office design. Established in 1985, the firm provides comprehensive purchasing, remodeling, and contracting services, as well as detailed on-site supervision and project management of all construction tasks. It utilizes years of experience to create spaces that reflect their clients' personal taste and preferences, while allowing for changing individual and family needs. Her work has been widely published.
• 522 S. Sepulveda Blvd., Suite 104, Los Angeles, California 90049
• 310.659.9203 • gij@earthlink.net
• www.ejaivinasid.com

Feinmann Inc. is known for its thoughtful and beautiful design, a well-articulated process, superb craftsmanship, responsive service, and the best value for the cost. With a little inspiration and a lot of follow-through, the Feinmann team has transformed hundreds of homes in the Boston area from good to great. With the client's personal style and budget clearly in mind, the firm produces distinctive designs that respect the beauty of the home's past while building in new functionality for the future. As specialists in whole house renovations, room additions, and kitchen/ bath remodels, the award-winning design/build team offers architectural design to furnishings selection.
• 27 Muzzey St., Lexington, Massachusetts 02421
• 781.860.9800 • info@feinmann.com
•www.feinmann.com

Established in 1994, **FORMA Design**'s multi-disciplinary approach results in high quality, concept-driven design solutions that efficiently and effectively maximize the client's time and financial resources. It addresses architecture, interiors, and graphic communications issues to provide "integrated design" solutions. It has received numerous local, regional and national awards;

been published extensively in a number of publications; and featured on TV. Andre Charalambous, AIA, IIDA, Principal, combines over twenty years of experience in architecture and interior architecture with his deep interest in all aspects of design and a career in painting and photography.
• 1524 U St. NW, Ste 2, Washington, DC
• 202.265.2625 • mail@formaonline
• www.formaonline.com

Garden Accents was inspired by Elizabeth Schumacher's appreciation for the importance of ornaments in good garden design and her world-wide search for quality pieces for her own award-winning garden. Founded in 1979, Garden Accents offers original art, antiques, and contemporary ornaments from the United States, Europe, Africa, and Asia. Voted "Best of Philly," Garden Accents has an inventory of over five thousand pieces and will also help design and install custom and commissioned work.
• 4 Union Hill Rd., West Conshohocken, Pennsylvania 19428
• 610.825.5525 • www.gardenaccents.com

Glen Irani, Principal of **Glen Irani Architects,** developed his knowledge of highly exclusive contemporary residential design during his employment at the studio of John Lautner FAIA and later at Richard Meier and Partners. In 1994, he began his own practice with a focus on contemporary residential, commercial, and cultural projects for clients who are committed to creating unique contemporary environments that respond to their lives as well as the physical and cultural context in which they reside. The work of Glen Irani Architects has been widely exhibited and published worldwide.
• 410 Sherman Canal Venice, California 90291
• 310.305.8840 • 310.822.1801
•www.glenirani.com

Hays + Ewing Design Studio (HEDS) is a full-service architecture and planning firm recently formed by architects Christopher Hays and Allison Ewing, who have over 40 years of combined experience in designing award-winning commercial, cultural, residential, institutional, and planning projects. US Green Building Council LEED-accredited professionals, its principals bring expertise in incorporating aesthetic and ecological considerations in a range of building scales and types in projects located around the globe. They believe good design merges beautiful solutions with ecological integrity and seek to achieve this goal in all their projects.
• 609 East Market St., Suite 203, Charlottesville, Virginia, 22902
• 434. 979.3222• aewing@hays-ewing.com
• www.hays-ewing.com

Darryl Tucker, ASID, CID, is the owner of **Helicon Hall Design Associates**, a full service interior design firm with a specialty in lighting design. Tucker has designed numerous residential and commercial projects, ranging from residential homes and condominiums to offices and banquet facilities. Her work has been featured in numerous publications and received awards.
• 2100 Linwood Ave., Fort Lee, New Jersey 07024
• 201. 944.1212 • heliconhalldesign@earthlink.net

Jonathan B. Isleib LLC was founded in 2004 by visionary Connecticut designer Jonathan Isleib. For more than 35 years, Isleib has been designing for residential, institutional, and commercial clients. With a repertoire that includes both innovative new construction and meticulous restorations, Isleib is perhaps best known for designs that bear a symbiotic relationship with nature. Many publications have featured his work. His firm provides expertise in all aspects of design, from landscape to architecture, space planning to furniture. Prior to founding Jonathan B. Isleib LLC, Isleib spent 31 years as the founding partner of Interdesign Limited.
• 268 Joshuatown Rd., Lyme, Connecticut 06371
• 860. 526.5577 • jonathan@jbidesign.com

Kerrie Kelly IIDA ASID CID Certified Interior Designer #6031 and ASID California Central/Nevada Chapter Past-President, has designed prestigious homes and created the interiors of model homes throughout northern California and Nevada. In 1995, she founded All American Design & Furnishings, Inc. The firm's goal for every project is to capture the client's own style through a process of exposure, education, and creativity. The firm is experienced in both commercial and residential projects.
• 136 Crow Canyon Dr., Folsom, California 95630
• 916.919.3023 • kerriek@sbcglobal.net

Keogh Design, Inc., founded in 1988 by Charlene Keogh, is best known for high-end residential interiors tailored to each individual client. With design projects throughout the United States, the firm is famous for its timeless and unique furniture and product designs. Ms. Keogh has received AIA's Excellence in Interiors Award and brings to her clients a lively mix of creativity, passion, and fun in combination with a pragmatic business approach. The firm's work has been featured in numerous publications, including *Interior Design, Design Times*, and *Dwell* magazines.
• 180 Duane St., New York, New York
• 212.964.4170• ck@keoghdesign.com
• www.keoghdesign.com

Magdalena Keck Interior Design is a Manhattan-based design house focused on interior contemporary design. The firm's versatile projects include luxury residences, specialty shops, and restaurants. Inspired by nature, art, and technology, Keck's signature approach combines immaculate craftsmanship and function to achieve a distinctive elegance through honest, clean, and genuine design. Her streamlined designs have been published, and she has been featured among forty established and up and coming New York designers in the book *Spectacular Homes of Metro New York*.
• 12 West 27th St., 10th Floor, New York, NY10001
• 212.725.7704 • mkeck@magdalenakeck.com
• www.magdalenakeck.com

Maryann Thompson, a member of Harvard University's Architecture faculty, founded **Maryann Thompson Architects** in 2000. Her architectural investigations revolve around such concerns as the creation of a rich and thoughtful edge between inside and outside, utilizing light as a material, and employing warm, natural materials in order to accentuate a sense of place. Thompson carries degrees in both architecture and landscape architecture, bringing to her practice an interdisciplinary approach, where issues of site and landscape are central to design thinking. Her work has been widely published and received numerous awards and honors, including two AIA National Honor and numerous AIA New England awards.
• 14 Hillside Ave., Cambridge, Massachusetts 02140
• 617.491.4144 • maryann@maryannthompson.com
• www.maryannthompson.com

Miriam Ansell Interiors has worked with clients in New York City, New Jersey, Connecticut, and Pennsylvania.

Specializing in simple solutions that give maximum impact, she has developed a reputation for achieving a sense of balance, beauty, and harmony in her interiors. As she guides her clients through the design process, she seeks out the very best solutions—from the showrooms of New York to places as far flung as Venice, Jerusalem, Hong Kong, Cambodia, and India. Her designs have appeared in a wide range of publications.
• New York, New York 10001 • 212.221.6411
• New Hope, Pennsylvania 18938 • 215.862.3780
• design@miriamansellinteriors.com
• www.miriamansellinteriors.com

Nicole Hogarty Designs (NHD) is a full service residential interior design and consultation firm, servicing New England and New York. From design concept to project completion, NHD is committed to a design approach that engages each client as a participant in the process. The firm takes pride in designing personalized spaces that reflect the homeowner's lifestyle and vision, and its environments offer a seamless blend of color and texture, energized with unexpected elements. It works to discover and reveal the individual identity of each home, ensuring a design that is both beautiful and functional.
• 158 Gentian Ave., Providence, Rhode Island 02908
• 401.831.7878 • info@nicolehogartycom
• www.nicolehogarty.com

Jacquie Germany, the principal designer at **Nina's Nuances Interior Design Inc.**, was educated in industrial hygiene and environmental sciences as well as interior design. Currently, she finds that many of her residential clients are looking to implement OSHA and EPA regulations in the home. Consequently, she is designing ergonomic, environmentally friendly, and aesthetically pleasing environments for her clients.
• 218 Bloomfield Ave., Montclair, New Jersey 07042
• 973.233.1226 • jacquie@ninasnuances.com
• www.ninasnuances.com

Robert Harvey Oshatz, Architect, states that his relationship with his clients is based on a mutual understanding that architecture is the synthesis of logic and emotion. "The architect is the client's artist, creator, logician of an evolving aesthetic structure; a designer of not only the visual but also internal space. My commitment is to interpret the individual poetic sense of each building site with my client's functional, emotional and spiritual needs. The challenge is to translate that spirit into architectural poetry. When an emotional idea is taken to its logical conclusion, a structure reflecting the client's dream and fantasies is brought into reality."
• PO Box 19091, Portland, Oregon 97219
• 503.635.4243 • robert@oshatz.com
• www.oshatz.com

Joan Grabel, award-winning landscape designer, is president of **Park Slope Design**, a landscape design company that is committed to sustainable practices and responsible design. Specializing in custom residential designs integrating landscape and architecture, Grabel approaches landscape design with an artist's sensibility and works closely with clients to actualize their vision. A featured landscape designer on Home and Garden Television, her designs have been featured in numerous publications.
• 3940 Laurel Canyon Blvd.,#173, Studio City, California 91604
• 818.788.4312 • parkslopedesign@aol.com
•www.parkslopedesign.net

Established in 1992 by Bill Reid, **Remodel West** is a seventeen-year-old Northern California company specializing in the design and construction of residential remodel projects ranging from kitchens and bath to additions and new homes. It functions as two separate firms, Remodel West Design Inc. and Remodel West Construction Inc., allowing the firm to fulfill projects from the professional design community and clients desiring design and construction. It focuses on implementing sustainable design and material solutions for all its projects. Its capabilities include performing all design duties required to obtain necessary building permits and completion of construction—all by its own staff.
•12333 Saratoga Sunnyvale Rd., Saratoga, California 95070
• 408.257.4900 • breid@remodelwest.com
• www.remodelwest.com

Rios Clementi Hale Studios creates buildings, places, and products that are thoughtful, effective, and beautiful. Established in 1985, this extraordinary practice has developed an international reputation for its collaborative and multi-disciplinary approach, establishing an award-winning tradition across an unprecedented range of design disciplines. The firm's architecture, landscape architecture, planning, urban, interior, exhibit, graphic, and product designers delight in projects as diverse as a new headquarters for The California Endowment, to the Terminator2 3D attraction at Universal City, to numerous private residences. The firm has received national and local AIA and ASLA awards and been recognized for its work in graphics, furniture, and interior design.
• 639 N Larchmont Blvd., Los Angeles, California 90004
• 323.785.1800
• www.rchstudios.com

The work of **SsD** explores a version of sustainability that approaches design as a convergent, interdisciplinary venture. In this light, an economy of means is favored over an additive and redundant methodology: Instead of separating aspects of architecture, landscape, history, social systems, and codes into their constituent disciplines, these agendas are simultaneously explored so that minimum form can take maximum effect. Because this approach is inherently based on finding solutions that minimize material and energy use while maximizing performance, sustainability emerges as an integrated result. Along with being published in major media, SsD has received many prestigious design awards and lectured and exhibited at many universities and conferences.
• 171 Brookline Street, Cambridge, Massachusetts 02139
• 325 w 38th Street, Suite 208, New York, New York 10018
• 212. 248. 7500 • info@ssdarchitecture.com
• www.ssdarchitecture.com

Studio H+L is an architecture and design firm that works on both residential and commercial projects. While the two partners (and spouses), Lina Husodo and James Linville, have been involved in projects throughout the United States, Studio H+L's work has concentrated on the central Texas region. Their work has been included in several AIA Austin Homes Tours, as well as numerous publications and TV.
• 3307 Windy Harbor Drive, Austin, Texas 78734
• 512.478.9828 • studiohl@austin.rr.com
• www.studioHplusL.com

A passion for regional architecture, exotic artifacts, fabrics, and colors is what defines Danielle Orlowski,

designer and owner of **Tastefully Yours Design Studio**. She draws from an international education, extensive travel, and architectural experience to bring global style home to her clients. She likes to incorporate Asian pieces in a traditional setting. She believes each room has its own story. Whether building a new home or remodeling a single room, Danielle and her team of designer professionals strive to create living spaces that suit a client's lifestyle and invoke a sense of harmony and peace.
• 201.389.6707 • danielle@tydesignstudio.com

Nancy Taylor, Allied Member ASID, established **Taylor Interior Design, Inc**. in 1967. Today, Taylor leads an experienced team of highly qualified design professionals and support staff specializing in high end residential and commercial interiors throughout the country. For every project, she aims to achieve a level of design that will look and feel comfortable for at least twenty years, believing that, with good design, the whole becomes greater than the sum of its parts. The firm stands by a philosophy of timeless, sophisticated design that reflects the client's point of view. Its work has figured in numerous publications.
• 125 Benefit St., Providence, Rhode Island 02903
• 401.274.1232 • nancy@taylorinteriordesign.com
• www.taylorinteriordesign.com

Teal Michel ASID provides symmetry, detailing, and quality of products. She creates remarkable interior spaces that speak to their owners. A native of the Northeast, her work is cosmopolitan yet comfortably livable. Her trademark is impeccable style and professionalism in every project she designs—big or small.
• 3736 Surry Ridge Ct., Charlotte, North Carolina 28210
• 704.554.7036 • tealmichel@juno.com
• www.tealmichelasid.com

Reginald L. Thomas Architect, AIA, LLC specializes in historically based, high-end, residential work. His work has been featured in several prestigious publications, and he is actively involved with the Historic Preservation Committee of his town. He believes that all aspects of design, exterior and interior, should be fully explored in order to come to a unique and complete solution. Each project is approached in a comprehensive, professional manner through successful collaboration with contractors, interior designers, landscape architects, artisans, and craftsmen, and the clients' needs, budget, and time limitations are of equal importance.
• 415 Madison Ave, 14th Floor, New York, New York 10017
• 908.412.8373 • reginaldthomas@ritarch.com

For 40 years, **TruexCullins** of Burlington, Vermont, has played a vital role in creating buildings that contribute lasting value to their inhabitants and communities. Its record and reputation testify to its excellence in designing structures that integrate harmoniously with their natural and built surroundings. It strives to create beautiful design solutions that are safe, flexible, comfortable, efficient, and durable, focusing on "less flashy" construction and design issues such as a sound building envelope, the use of renewable fuels (wind, hydro, biomass), water conservation, proper site placement and building orientation, and the effective use of existing space within renovated buildings.
• 209 Battery St., Burlington, Vermont 05401
• 802.658.2775 • architects@truexcullins.com
• www.truexcullins.com

Webber+Studio's award-winning work has been inspired by North America's traditions. Whether prefabricated metal buildings, suburban tract homes, or even the more refined folk styles, modernism, and minimalism, the studio's work is influenced by the artistry displayed in these various mediums. Being less concerned with style than function and context, David Webber treats each project as a study in joining his client's objectives with the characteristics of their program and site to achieve the uniqueness that is the hallmark of his work. Webber's architectural vision has been highlighted in numerous print and broadcast media.
• 300 West Ave., Suite 1322, Austin, Texas 78701
• 512.236.1032 • info@webberstudio.com
• www.webberstudio.com

David Wright has designed over 500 passive solar and alternative construction buildings, both residential and commercial/institutional. Today, he focuses on the innovative integration of advanced building materials along with passive solar and solar electric technologies into mainstream architectural environmental design. Nationally certified as an architect, he is licensed to practice in several states and can work throughout the United States as well as overseas. He has been published in many periodicals and books, received many design awards, and lectured throughout the United States and Europe. His work has been exhibited at several international exhibits as well as the Smithsonian Institute.
• 563-B Idaho Maryland Rd., Grass Valley, California 95945
• 530.477.5057 • dwright@netshel.net
• www.dwrightaia.com

Other Resources

Tuulikki Loring's work is characterized by warmth, charm, color, and idiosyncratic choice. In business since 1985, she had designed both contemporary and traditional interiors. Her strength is her Finnish heritage, her use of design and color, and her combinations of antiques with contemporary china and glassware.
• 33 Bloomfield St., Lexington, Massachusetts 02421
• 781.862.4672 • tuulikki@rcn.com

A direct importer, **Pan Zhai** is a significant source for Asian home decor. Designers and homeowners from Boston to New York use it as a source for classic Chinese country antiques, reproductions, and unique artifacts. Its owners travel to China several times each year and welcome special requests.
• 940 Waterman Ave., East Providence, Rhode Island 02914
• 401.435.6888 • info@panzhai.com
• www.panzhai.com

Tricia Traxler uses color and art to enliven the world. With a pronounced international flair, Tricia creates a look that will last for years. She also consults on garden design.
• Winchester, Massachusetts
• 781.721.2489• ttraxler@verizon.net

Bibliography

Adamson, Paul, Marty Arbunich and Earnest Braun. *Eichler: Modernism Rebuilds the American Dream*. Layton, Utah: Gibbs Smith, 2002

Black, Alexander and Noboru Murata. *The Japanese House: Architecture and Interiors*. North Clarendon, Vermont: Tuttle Publishing, 2000

Freeman, Michael. *The New East.* New York, New York: Rizzoli International Publications, Inc. 2007

Master Lam Kam Chuen. *Feng Shui Handbook*. New York, New York: Henry Holt Reference Book, 1996

Riley, Terrence and Peter Reed. [Ed.]. *Frank Lloyd Architect.* New York, New York: MOMA. 1994

"Frank Gehry's Japan. A Private Tour of the Architect's Inspirations and Aesthetic Touchstones," *Architectural Digest.* May 2006

"Japanese Style House," *Architectural Digest.* July 1993

Index